A WAY IN THE WORLD

A Way in the World

Family Life as Spiritual Discipline

ERNEST BOYER, Jr.

Harper & Row, Publishers, San Francisco
Cambridge, Hagerstown, New York, Philadelphia
1817 London, Mexico City, São Paulo, Singapore, Sydney

FIRST EDITION

Library of Congress Cataloging in Publication Data

Boyer, Ernest.
    A WAY IN THE WORLD.

    1. Spirituality. 2. Family—Religious life.
3. Boyer, Ernest. I. Title.
BV4501.2.B684   1984   249   84-48983
ISBN 0-06-061032-8

---

84 85 86 87 88 10 9 8 7 6 5 4 3 2 1

Pamela—

   for you, of course

Contents

Acknowledgments

There are so many people who had a part in this book. Only a few can be mentioned here.

First to be thanked must be my parents, Ernest and Kathryn Boyer, Sr. I thank them for the help and encouragement they have provided throughout my life and for the special contribution they have made here. It was they who made this book possible, not only by helping in concrete ways when special needs arose, but, more importantly, by giving me a vision from childhood of what a marvelous spiritual gift family life can be.

Also important to this process was Dr. Sharon Parks of Harvard Divinity School. It was her inspired lectures that led me to ask the questions that drew me into the research, the introspection, and the discovery that produced this book; and it was she who read so much of my work in its earliest stages and encouraged me to continue. She is a truly gifted teacher.

I want also to thank the people of the communities I visited, especially those of Open House Community, Reba Place Fellowship, and the New Jerusalem Community, for sharing so much with me.

A very special thanks must also be given to two people whose lives are such an important part of this book, William Boyer (1872 –1972), my great-grandfather, and Sarah Spampinato, my wife's grandmother. I am only one of the many people their lives have touched.

I am also grateful to my editors. I want especially to thank John Loudon, who saw what this book could be and helped me to see it, too. In addition, I thank Kathy Reigstad for her help with the text, and also my father-in-law, Anthony G. Napier, for his assistance in proofreading and correcting.

I would like to acknowledge my debt to the people and staff of St. Ann's Parish in Somerville, Massachusetts. Not only did they provide a physical home—an unusual one—by letting my family and me live in their empty convent while I worked there as a lay minister; they gave me a spiritual home, too. I want to thank particularly the Rev. Francis O'Hare, pastor, and Sr. Dorothy Welch for the inspiration their vision and compassion have brought me, but also Rev. Neil Mullaney, Meg Anzalone, and Rev. Angelo Loscocco for the help and support they have given.

Thanks as well to *Sojourners* magazine, where an early version of Part I appeared as the articles "The Magnificent Dance" and "Edges and Rhythms" (in the June and July issues, 1984).

And finally there is my wife, Pamela. I thank her especially for the courage and joy she brings to the life we share. Drawing together the spirituality of the desert and that of the edge is always an adventure. It is she who makes it fun.

Introduction

Two years ago I sat in a crowded room at Harvard Divinity School as Dr. Sharon Parks gave a talk on what she called the spirituality of the desert. This is a way of life that takes its name from those men and women among the early Christians who interpreted the gospel as a call to a life of solitary prayer, left the comfort of family and friends, the security of home and village, and set out to live alone in caves or small huts in the harsh Egyptian desert. As she described this life of deep commitment, solitude, prayer, and reflection, I felt its attraction and recognized my own need for a way of life something like this.

But I also felt something else—a sense of frustration. Married and the father of three small sons, I was deeply involved with the needs of my children and of the family as a whole. Was such a life possible with the commitment of a family?

The lecture ended. I sat still for a while and tried to draw my conflicting emotions together, then made my way to the front of the room.

Dr. Parks was putting away her notes. She looked up.

"Just one question," I said. "Is there childcare in the desert?"

This book is my attempt to answer my own question. It is part of what has been for me a long journey, one that took me to cities I had never before visited, to books I had not yet read, and to conversations with both friends and strangers. It also took me deep within myself. And from it all I found not only that there is in a certain sense childcare in the desert—there are ways, that is, in which those of us involved with families can come to know the exhilaration of that life of fullest searching and expression—but, even more important, I discovered the value of another spirituality which is uniquely its own, that of the family. I discovered that there are spiritual gifts to be found there that rival or better those of the desert. This book is the result of what I have learned of two ways of life, that of the desert and that of the family, or, as I prefer to call them, life on the edge and life at the center. It tells of what each separately has to offer and how they can be joined.

I. TWO WAYS OF LIFE

1. Life on the Edge

Dear God, kindle a fire in me, kindle it and let it burn to a white heat. Kindle a fire and let it rage inside me to feed itself on my bone and blood and sinew until I am consumed and only the fire remains. Turn my soul into a blaze, God, a blaze so bright and hot that it can be felt right through me to warm with your warmth all who come near.

Skellig Michael is a peak of bare stone rising hundreds of feet out of the cold Atlantic six miles off the western coast of Ireland. A rugged pinnacle of granite, it stands in defiance of both the distant mainland and the fierce lashings of the surf. Brutal and inaccessible, with cliffs rising to unlikely heights and then sloping steeply to precarious ledges, it seems unapproachable and uninhabitable, and yet for over one hundred years beginning in the sixth century a small group of Christian hermits made Skellig's Rock their home.

Eleven years ago I visited the spot. I had been sailing that summer with the merchant marine and had docked in Cork, Ireland. The ship would be in port only four days, but four days were all I needed. After a day and a half by train and car I found myself waiting on a dock as the sun rose and the fisherman and his son who were to take me and a dozen or so others tried to decide if the day was calm enough. The trip could only be made, they said, in the best of weather. At last they agreed that the trip could be made.

We climbed down a wooden ladder into an open fishing boat about twenty feet in length. There was just enough room for the twelve of us to stand. It was an hour before we had worked our way through the channel and out to open sea. The waves rose to heights of ten feet or more, so that, riding a crest, we seemed to rest atop a mountain, then slipping into a trough a moment later, to wallow in a valley made entirely of water.

One woman became ill. Cramped as we were, we huddled closer together to make room for her to stretch out on the deck. Two covered her with their coats.

It was another three hours before we neared the rock. As we approached, both the fisherman and his son became visibly more tense. The man maneuvered the boat toward a small opening in the side of the rock where a narrow cement dock had been built. The boy worked his way to the bow and crouched there, ready to spring, a coil of heavy rope in one hand. Slowly we drew closer until suddenly a wave took us; the man shut off the engine as the wave carried us forward toward the crevice in the stone. All at once the man shouted and the boy leapt from the boat and, just making the edge of the dock, ran beside us, then frantically lashed the rope around a mooring. The boat stopped abruptly, throwing us forward as the wave on which we rode surged ahead, shattering into spray on the rocks three yards beyond.

The fisherman told us we had three hours.

Following a trail rising higher and higher above the waves we came to the plateau on which were perched a half a dozen stone huts, the ruins of a tiny church, a Celtic cross carved in stone, an improvised terrace forming a small garden, and a graveyard—although the soil seemed hardly deep enough to cover the roots of plants, let alone the dead. No more than fifty feet from the last of the huts the plateau ended in a straight, vertical drop hundreds of feet to the rocks and waves below.

I walked from hut to hut, felt the soft, cold moss (apparently the only plant able to survive untended), stood beside the ancient graves, and paced out the ruins of the church. Finally the awesomeness of it made me stop. I looked all around; the dark sea was everywhere. I shivered from the wind—cold and wild even in August, it would be deadly in January. I looked back to the mainland, no more than a grey line on the horizon, then to the empty horizon to the west, where, as these hermits believed, the earth fell away.

These people lived on the edge, the edge of everything: the edge of a cliff, the edge of survival, the edge of the world, but perhaps

—and at that moment, for the first time in my life I could believe it—also at the edge of God.

But what did that mean, I asked myself throughout the four hours back to the mainland as the sky grew steadily darker and the wind more wild; what could it mean to live on the edge of God? Was it worth enduring all that I just saw? And what would push a man or woman to try?

But the answer to the last question I already knew, at least in part. What drew those men out onto that rock was something inside them that was incomplete, a longing for what was just beyond them, something they in no way understood, only partially perceived, and yet felt nearby. It was a longing to meet a deeper reality and by meeting it be transformed into something more than they were.

I too had felt this longing. Everyone does. The difficulty comes in recognizing it for what it is.

The men who had gone to that narrow peak of stone called Skellig Michael had not only recognized the longing but found one of the oldest and most universal ways to express it, one that, because it is so simple and so direct, has never lost its fascination. As Alfred North Whitehead writes:

The great religious conceptions which haunt the imaginations of civilized mankind are scenes of solitariness: Prometheus chained to his rock, Mohamet brooding in the desert, the meditations of the Buddha, the solitary Man on the Cross. It belongs to the depth of the religious spirit to have felt forsaken even by God.[1]

But to glimpse what it was that these men gained and what it was they suffered it is necessary to go elsewhere. I began to get an answer in Athanasius' *Life of Antony,* a biography of the fourth-century Egyptian hermit which, perhaps, these hermits of Skellig Michael had had a chance to read.

Antony was from a moderately wealthy Alexandrian family, but at eighteen both his parents died and he was left alone with a younger sister. In the months that followed he became more and more preoccupied with the fact that the apostles had forsaken everything to follow their Lord and, after hearing the verse from the Bible where Jesus tells the rich young man to sell his possessions and give the money to the poor, he did just that. Then, later, hearing the verse, "Do not be anxious about tomorrow," he resolved to do this as well; he put his sister in the care of nuns and went to live alone just outside of town. There his contact with people was restricted but regular.

It was then that he began to struggle with the doubts, uncertainties, and temptations that he was to know for so many years to come—temptations that to his eyes came in the form of demons. The struggle quickly became so torturous and so difficult that, "girding himself . . . Antony went out to the tombs that were situated some distance from the village,"[2] and shut himself inside, giving himself over solely to his fight.

The horror of his visions nearly killed him and when the friend who had gone with him opened the tomb several days later, he found him lying unconscious. But for the first time Antony felt he was gaining control. Alone, he went deeper into the desert, discovered a deserted fort, and barricaded himself inside. In that place he sought to find God and to overcome the demons that attacked him from all sides, demons that to the friends who would arrive to listen outside "sounded like clamoring mobs inside making noises, emitting pitiful sounds and crying out, 'Get away from what is ours! What do you have to do with the desert?' "[3]

The long struggle was rewarded.

Nearly twenty years he spent in this manner pursuing the ascetic life by himself, not venturing out and only occasionally being seen by anyone. After this, when many possessed the desire and will to emulate his asceticism, and some of his friends came and tore down and forcefully removed the fortress door, Antony came forth as though from some shrine, having been led into divine mysteries and inspired by God.[4]

Here, in this *Life of Antony* are the elements of what has been called the spirituality of the desert and what I call life on the edge. There is, first, a call; second, a gradual progression both in the understanding of the call and in its attainment; third, a struggle with demons—whatever form those "demons" might take; and, fourth, the vision—divine mysteries and inspiration.

First is the call. For Antony it came quite simply. He heard one passage from the Gospel and all the rest of his long life was a response to that passage. The passage was read in public and there were many others who heard it, but, for Antony, it was as if "the passage were read on his account,"[5] and nothing after that was exactly the same. For him the beginning was clearly marked. For most others, I suspect, it is far less distinct—a gradual awakening to a sense of incompleteness, an awareness of an absence, of something vacant and unfilled. And with this sensation comes a strange restlessness, an unarticulated longing for something that seems both unattainable and just within reach. It begins when a person is quite young and mounts steadily into a profound hunger for fulfillment and a search for the transcendent.

The feeling is universal. Everyone knows this longing to be more than he or she is, this longing that is in fact a primary religious urge and one just as basic to humankind as that of survival or sexuality. The problem is that it is seldom recognized for what it is. Instead, the sense of incompleteness is assumed to be a physical or material need. And because it is a need so widely misunderstood, ours has become a society that uses cars, homes, sexual encounters, and even food to fill the vacancy in our lives that these things simply cannot fill. Only when the need is identified for what it is, the searching of a creature who is incomplete, inadequate, and mortal for that which is complete, fulfilled, and immortal—the searching of the soul for God—only then can it begin to be satisfied. Then the call of the spirituality of the desert can be answered.

The second aspect of life on the edge is the gradual understanding of what exactly such a life involves. Antony did not answer the call by going directly into the desert, not at all. He moved out gradually, first selling a few of his possessions, then living at the edge of town, a while later moving out alone. When he went to lock himself inside the tombs he had a friend accompany him; later he went alone. Even the twenty years alone in the abandoned fort was only a stage of the journey, because he was later to go to even more secluded and desolate spots. The point is that a life lived on the edge must be done gradually, in stages.

Surely Moses, listening for the first time to the voice of the Lord in the burning bush, had only the faintest suspicion of the glory and the suffering of the exodus he was soon to be called to lead. And Jesus' disciples—would they have responded the way they did to his request to follow him if they had understood fully that the journey was to end at Calvary? The desert is harsh; its spirituality harsher still. God prepares those God calls to live there.

It is a life of total vulnerability. To surrender fully to that longing for transformation is to be willing to relinquish all that you are in order to become all that you can become. As Nikos Kazantzakis writes:

Three kinds of souls, three kinds of prayer:
1. I am a bow in your hands, Lord, draw me lest I rot.
2. Do not overdraw me, Lord, I shall break.
3. Overdraw me, Lord, and who cares if I break.[6]

To accept the spirituality of life on the edge is to become this third soul and pray this third prayer.

Life lived on the edge is also one of solitude. It is a life turned inward, a life alone. It is one where the surrender is so complete that the ego itself is offered as sacrifice. In so doing, the society most people crave as a buttress to their sense of individuality, uniqueness, and importance becomes incidental and ludicrous. It gets in the way. "Solitude is the furnace of transformation. Without solitude we remain victims of our society and continue to be entangled in the illusions of the false self."[7] In solitude the masks are burned away and the beliefs and self-delusions used to support the ambition and self-importance taken to be so central to our being are turned to ash. The furnace of solitude burns hot and brutally swift. In his novel *Nostromo* Joseph Conrad describes its effect on a young man named Decoud who by chance found himself stranded on a small island a few miles off the coast of South America.

Solitude from a mere outward condition of existence becomes very swift-ly a state of soul in which the affectations of irony and scepticism have no place. It takes possession of the mind and drives forth the thought into exile of utter unbelief. After three days of waiting for the sight of some human face, Decoud caught himself entertaining a doubt of his own in-dividuality.[8]

For Decoud the conflict was deadly. "Both his intelligence and his passion were swallowed up easily in this great unbroken solitude of waiting without faith."[9] After five days he pointed the pistol he carried to his heart and killed himself.

Standing high above the waves on Skellig Michael I wondered if any of those who lived there had ever responded as Decoud had done to the terrible power of solitude. Surely there had been those for whom it had been a temptation.

This is not a journey to be begun casually. And yet Whitehead says that "religion is what the individual does with his own solitariness"[10] and, further, that "religion is solitariness, and if you are never solitary, you are never religious,"[11] statements suggesting that there is something to be gained in solitude as well as suffered.

And what is gained can be awesome. For after the solitude has done its work, infected the soul with its fire, burned away irony and skepticism, burned away all feeling of self-importance, even all certainty of an individual existence, after it has grown into a raging conflagration as it feeds itself on hopes, ambitions, and be-liefs until all is gone, then suddenly the flames quiet and solitude becomes something extraordinary. To feel this is to feel the trans-formation, to know that nothing that was, continues and every-thing that is, is complete. It is to discover for the first time God's power and majesty, to find it at the very core of your own being.

But life on the edge is also one of death. As Dietrich Bonhoeffer writes, "When Christ calls a man, he bids him come and die."[12] This is more than a call to the death of the self; it is one that asks a person to discover physical death. That does not mean that life on the edge actively seeks death, but that it must, first, live with the constant vision of death's certainty—a vision everyone else tries to avoid—and, second, never shun death if it approaches. It is a life that can never compromise, so that if life lived anywhere else but on a rock six miles from the Irish coast would be a compromise, then it is to the rock you go, knowing full well you might not live to see another spring. And if it would be a compromise to go anywhere but with Jesus to Calvary, then it is to Calvary you go, fully aware that the person who might replace him on the cross might be you.

These then are the harsh elements of the life lived on the edge—the spirituality found in the desert or on Skellig Michael's rock, a spirituality where things that are gentle and easy have little place. It is the life begun by Moses when, alone in the desert herding his flocks, he heard the voice of the Lord in the burning bush. It is also the life begun by Jesus with forty days alone in the wilderness. It is, in short, the life of a prophet. From life lived on the edge comes an altered vision. After making a "clean break with [the] conventional, accepted social context in order to swim for one's life into an apparently irrational void,"[13] nothing seems quite the same, either in the world as a whole or in the community of human beings. The confined sight of humanity has been exchanged for the wider vision of one who knows God, and to have this vision is to see great value in things ignored or scorned by nearly everyone else while recognizing how little true worth there is in nearly everything others take as important.

To see in this way is a disturbing experience both for the person with the prophetic vision and for the community upon which he or she gazes. Seeing the falseness of so much that is done, the prophet might speak it, or, more disturbing still, not speak it but simply live in a way that offers a glimpse at what he or she has found, and so threaten what is familiar with what is better. Even if the community tries to understand, it will not be able to, not fully. The problem is that a prophet standing before the people can tell of his or her vision, but not give the vision itself. For that they too must go into the desert.

But the vision of life on the edge is not solely that of the prophet. It is also that of the artist. Thus it is that a young boy named David, tending his sheep alone in the desert as Moses had done, also came into the presence of God. But what he heard in that encounter was not a command to liberation, but the melody of a song, a song to which he gave voice. To live a life on the edge may result in a call to lead others and bring them freedom, or it may be a call to die for others and bring them life, but it may also be a call to sing for others and bring them peace. Anyone embarking on a life lived on the edge must be prepared for each of these—or perhaps for all together.

Anyone living life on the edge will meet with inner demons. With no barriers to separate a person from him- or herself, all the powers of the unconscious rage forth. For Antony they took hideous forms—devils, wild beasts, reptiles. They came as men and women whispering obscenities or arguing calmly that what he was doing was senseless. For others they may take less tangible forms, embodied simply in the fatigue of the effort or as emptiness, fear, or doubt.

Antony himself summarized the effect. No matter how they come, the demons met in the life lived on the edge cause

terror of soul, confusion and disorder of thoughts, dejection, enmity toward ascetics, listlessness, grief, memory of relatives, and fear of death; and finally there is craving for evil, contempt for virtue, and instability of character.[14]

It is right to call these demons. They cannot be passed off as moods, a simple dipping of the mercury of emotions. These are powerful forces; for them to take control may mean destruction, madness, or death. They are a part of the life itself and of the loneliness and uncertainty that accompany it.

But the most powerful demons of life on the edge are not those that seek to push a person away from it, but those that seek to draw him or her too close. "We ought to understand this," Athanasius quotes Antony as saying, "the demons were not created as figures we now identify as 'demon,' for God made nothing bad. They were made good, but falling from the heavenly wisdom . . . they meddle with all things in their desire to frustrate our journey into heaven."[15] And so one of the greatest dangers of solitude can be solitude itself. When solitude reaches the point where, far from being a burden, it is preferred to anything else, then it has become destructive. Even the call to death, that other aspect of life on the edge, can become an attraction that, rather than expanding the soul, diminishes it. Life on the edge can show us something of the transcendent, and death as part of that transcendence, so that as we feel ourselves less and less attached to the finite, death begins to develop a fascination and attraction in itself. Such a person then comes under the spell of death.

He becomes an outcast of life, a man who seems doomed, fated to die, and at the same time a visionary, able to see into the future, a man of foreboding, looking forward to death and calamity, a man with an otherworldly air, an otherworldly charm. To break the spell of death he must embrace a finite existence. It is the dread of death that prevents him from acting, from taking risks involved in action. It is the fascination with death that prevents him from loving, from giving himself fully to life. To act, to love he must somehow overcome the dread, the fascination. In breaking the spell, nevertheless, he could lose everything he has gained from death. In ceasing to be an outcast of life, a doomed and fated man, he could become a tame man, a domesticated man.[16]

Nothing is as far from the goal of life on the edge as domestication, and yet nothing is as great a danger as losing the ability to love.

The conclusion seems to be that demons are a necessary part of life on the edge. They tear away complacency and make it far more difficult to turn an acceptance of solitude and death into a destructive fascination with them. In the stories of the Desert Fathers, those men who, for several hundred years after Antony, emulated his life in the desert, there is one concerning Abbot John the Dwarf who prayed to the Lord that his passion be taken from him. His prayer was granted

so that he became impassible. And in this condition he went to one of the elders and said: You see before you a man who is completely at rest and has no more temptations. The elder said: Go and pray to the Lord to command some struggle to be stirred up in you, for the soul is matured only in battles. And when the temptations started up again he did not pray that the struggle be taken away from him, but only said: Lord, give me strength to get through the fight.[17]

It is this courage that prays to meet the demons, not avoid them, that is one of the most extraordinary strengths of life on the edge. It is a courage that will always stand to meet the evils of the world, like the one that enabled the theologian Dietrich Bonhoeffer to stand up against the Nazis even though he risked and later suffered death in a prison camp. It is also a courage willing to meet the demons within. It is this courage that causes a person to pray Kazantzakis' third prayer.

But, finally, there is the reward of this harsh life on the edge, the vision of God's presence. "I pray thee," Moses dared to say to God, "show me thy glory."[18] And God did. When Moses was alone on the desert mountaintop of Sinai, God came to him and Moses had to cover his eyes, since to see the face of God would be to die, but he raised his head as God passed and saw the majesty of the Divine. And when he came down from the mountain the people stood back in fear. "Moses did not know that the skin of his face shone because he had been talking with God."[19]

And Antony, too, after his years alone in the desert had the mark of one who had come close to God.

It was not his physical dimensions that distinguished him from the rest, but the stability of character and the purity of the soul. His soul being free of confusion, he held his outer senses also undisturbed, so that from the soul's joy his face was cheerful as well, and from the movements of the body it was possible to sense and perceive the stable condition of the soul.[20]

As with Moses, here was a person through whom God could be seen. "His speech was seasoned with divine salt, so that no one resented him—on the contrary, all who came to him rejoiced over him."[21]

This is the human gentleness that comes of having seen God's majesty and lived, though living now transformed. What is seen is the God of fire, the God of the whirlwind, the God who creates and destroys, who builds up and tears down, who gives life and takes it back again—the God to whom Jesus prayed in the Garden of Gethsemane asking to have the burden of his suffering lifted from him and who answered no. It is this God, awesome and terrifying, who, once met, reveals that within it all—the building and the unbuilding, the growth and the decay, the life and the death—there is one great harmony, one vast, all-encompassing love far, far beyond the comprehension of any one human being, yet one that will reach out to that human being and so make despair indistinguishable from ecstasy and make solitude into space infinitely filled. This is the God met in the desert, on Skellig Michael, or in any life lived on the edge.

The price of this life is surrender, solitude, and death; the reward is the presence of God. The price is high, but there is nothing more magnificent than what it buys.

2. Life at the Center

Lord, grant that I never shun the pain of giving birth to love, nor the fatigue of the effort that nurtures it from day to day. Teach me to value each moment as I value each beat of my own heart, and to find in the pulsing of my blood that distant tempo of birth, of growth, of love and of death which repeats itself over and over through a billion hearts and a million years, and which is the echo of the one eternal rhythm.

I hold before my mind two images. The first is of a man wearing rough clothing cut from the hide of animals he himself has killed with stone-tipped spears. He is in a cave in one of the valleys in southern France that is sheltered from the fiercest cold of the Ice Age. The man is squatting on the floor of the cave, crouching near a fire he has built. He is mixing pigments—deep ochres, purples, reds, greens—grinding them from minerals gathered just now within the cave. As he grinds each into a powder he arranges them along the ground, then stands and studies the wall. There, drawn with the same deep colors he has just prepared, are the representations of the animals he knows well, the bison, the antelope, and others. The pictures have been there since the time of his father, and the time of his grandfather—in fact as long as anyone can remember. And now, just as his father had done and his grandfather before him, the man takes the pigment and, blowing the colorful dust through a hollow reed, redraws the pictures, tracing them as carefully as he can, matching color for color. When he is finished the pictures look as they did before, only brighter, fuller, renewed. Now the man places his hand against one of the few remaining empty spaces on the wall and, blowing pigment against it, leaves a mark, his imprint. With that he is finished. Leaving the fire to burn down, he returns to the mouth of the cave.

The second image is of a woman giving birth. She has been in labor for many hours. The regular pulsations of pain have been growing closer and closer and mounting in intensity, but they have long since blurred for her into one endless agony. For over an hour she has been nearly delirious, tossing her head back and forth wildly, and breaking groans with frantic screams so that the man waiting outside looks through the door only to be motioned angrily away by the two women called in to help. Suddenly something in the quality of the pain changes in a way that startles her, making her at once more alert. The women recognize the motion and arrange a blanket on the floor, helping her into a squatting position. Her face suddenly brilliant with sweat, she groans, pants, and rocks back and forth as she pushes as hard as she can. And suddenly the baby is born. It is a little boy, and he begins to cry as the midwives cut the cord and hand him to his mother, who is trembling and exhausted, but jubilant. She puts him to her breast. The women motion to the man outside. He enters the room pale, also trembling. Sitting down with the others he can say nothing and is silent while the midwives tidy up and chatter. At last one of them asks him what name he will choose for the baby. He can only nod toward the woman. It is she who says, "The name was chosen for us. He is to be called Jesus."

The first image is from the beginning of the human story, the second from the beginning of the Christian one. Together they represent the range of a second spirituality, that of the family. This spirituality is more common than that of the desert, but also more difficult to appreciate. It is one that can apply to any group formed to give care and love, but it applies most especially to that small unit made up of a man and a woman and their children. Like the spirituality of the desert, it has its rewards, its touch with the divine, and of these the first image hints. It also has its trials and suffering, these suggested by the second image. And like the spirituality of the desert it also has four aspects, the same four: the calling, the journey, the demons and, finally, the discovery of God.

There is, first, the calling. The twelve men who, became Jesus' disciples were not the only ones called to serve him, and their life of discipleship not the only one Jesus asked for. There was another as well. To this other life were called Mary and Joseph. This call sounded different from the other. There was for one thing less free choice. When Jesus asked his disciples to follow him, any one of them might have refused. But when the angel came to Mary and later to Joseph and told them that there was soon to be a child born to them, there was only one answer for them to give.

It is also a call to a different sort of life. Theirs was not a call so much to renunciation or deprivation as to hardship and routine. It was a call to form love into flesh and bone, then care for it and help it grow.

The disciples were called to follow Jesus, Mary and Joseph were called to feed him; the disciples were called to learn from Jesus, Mary and Joseph to teach him to speak; the disciples to stand beside him, Mary and Joseph to help him to stand. The disciples were called to suffer with Jesus the pain of his death so that he might give the gift of life. Mary and Joseph were called to suffer for him the pain of birth so that he might give the gift of love.

The spirituality of the family is, then, a calling; it is also a spiritual journey. If the spirituality of life on the edge must follow Antony's pattern of a slow progression further and further away from people and closer and closer to the presence of God, so too is this spirituality marked by a halting progression, but its progression is nearer and nearer to people and a gradual recognition of the love that marks God's presence there.

It begins with marriage. Although it is not always easy to recognize it as such, marriage is the most remarkable and most courageous of all human acts—the promise of two human beings to share life together on all levels, physical, economic, spiritual—a promise made in the face of the certainty of death, the certainty of change, and the uncertainty of everything else. There is nothing else a human being might choose to do that is quite like this act, nothing so foolish or so profound.

Marriage can be the most intense of all spiritual communities. In the *Symposium* Plato has Socrates advance a theory that humanity comes to know the divine only by degrees. It begins as physical love, an unashamedly sexual craving of one person for another.

From this physical love gradually develops another, a love for the person as a human being. This in time deepens so that, the first two remaining undiminished, a third love is formed—that for the other as an embodiment of the divine. From this flowers a love for the Divine itself. This is precisely the sort of discovery of God that marriage allows.

From the first attraction, the love of a man and woman deepens in the early days of a marriage into a profoundly formed union, a bonding of thought, hope, and need so uniform that each soul comes to reflect the image of the other. Like two suns orbiting about each other, it is a brilliant time, an all-embracing time, a time apart. It is a time of such beauty that when it passes—and it must pass—it might seem a loss. But what replaces it is something more profound, and in its own way more lovely still.

This next phase is a harder time, fragmented, fractured, often weighted with fatigue. These are what Anne Morrow Lindbergh, in her book *Gift from the Sea,* calls

the middle years of marriage . . . the struggle of life itself. [It is like] the oyster [which] has fought to have that place on the rock to which it has fitted itself perfectly and to which it clings tenaciously. So most couples in the growing years of marriage struggle to achieve a place in the world. It is a physical and material battle first of all, for a home, for children, and for a place in their particular society. In the midst of such a life there is not much time to sit facing one another over a breakfast table.[1]

For any marriage this is a dangerous time. The exhilaration of the first period is gone and the rewards of this one are not always apparent. This is a time when one of the marriage partners may buckle under the strain of the struggle, flounder in doubts and uncertainties, and need for a time to lean against the other for support. Later the role may be reversed and the other partner may in turn fall prey to worries, failures, and depression and so need to be carried by the first. In these periods the one doing the supporting may begin to think, "I am not being helped by this person, only held back," but because of that foolish, extraordinary vow, keep going. There are very few marriages lasting any length of time where both husband and wife do not have several opportunities to play out for each other both sides of the story of the good Samaritan; the one who at one time plays the part of the man broken and beaten along the road, the man who must be carried away, bandaged, and cared for, will a few years later be the one who must stop, slow his or her own journey, and help the other.

And so after the intensity of the early years, and in the midst of the struggle of the middle years, when both partners in the marriage believe they have seen every one of their spouse's many faces, they see two more—that of the afflicted and that of the comforter of the afflicted. And only after seeing both of those faces on the same person and knowing that they themselves had worn them as well, can each begin to really understand the nature of the divine. A love first born in an erotic attraction, nurtured in the intensity of the relationship that follows, matures through the ordinary pains and sharing of day-to-day life into a love very close to God's own.

Marriage is, then, very much a spiritual journey. So also is its most extraordinary result, parenthood.

To become a parent is to form the most intimate of all covenants with God. Abraham's original covenant with God was first of all a promise that he and Sarah would have a child; everything else followed upon this. And so too the new covenant, begun when the angel appeared to Mary and later to Joseph and announced the coming birth of Jesus. Both couples, Abraham and Sarah and Mary and Joseph, were given essentially the same message: first, that they were to have a child, and, second, that through their relationship with this child their relationship to God would deepen profoundly.

In this the births of Isaac and Jesus are identical to that of every child. With each baby born a private, intensely personal bond is formed between the parents and God, one weighted with burdens, but also with quiet gifts.

Parenthood can be seen as the fullest expression of a second essential human need. It is the need to love and nurture another, and it is just as strong and just as basic as that relentless spiritual hunger I have called longing for God. As Elizabeth O'Connor states in *The New Community:*

The spiritual law at the core of our being requires that we reach out. We are fulfilled to the extent that we are in relationship. We cannot disobey or even resist this law without suffering. So wondrously are we made that we are happiest when we are loving and miserable when we are not loving.[2]

The need of the parents to care for their child is as strong as the child's need to receive their care. It is for this reason that being a parent can be so painful as the child grows older. The child's need to receive diminishes, or at least becomes less pronounced, while the parent's need to give does not. Gifts of care and protection must be regretfully withheld or offered in more subtle ways.

Every child needs to receive love, but as a child grows into an adult he or she needs to give it as well. As with a tree that throughout the spring has drawn nourishment from the soil and sun and passes into summer heavy with fruit, there comes a human season when men and women draw from themselves a love that has grown to fullness and offer it back by placing it with another to grow, develop, and in turn be offered. The need is universal. But like that other human need, the longing for the transcendent, the need to love may not be recognized for what it is. It may be stunted, twisted, or stifled altogether. To be denied the opportunity to achieve the summer of this human season and so turn away the call to love is to suffer a great loss.

The covenant of parenthood has other aspects as well. It can be in its own way a vision for a world remade. With every family, human society has a chance to begin anew, to start again and correct the mistakes that went before. Every set of parents have the opportunity to work together to form a model for a better world and create in microcosm a new community. All parents are, then, potentially "builders of liberating communities that free love in [themselves] and free love in others."[3]

A third aspect of the covenant of parenthood is personal growth. Children grow, of course, but parents grow too, although for parents the growth is less obvious, frequently tedious, and usually difficult. All the lessons of parenthood spring from the hard work of loving. I have often suspected that all that occurs in childhood, all the awkwardness of the adolescent years, all the delicate maturation of early adulthood—all of that apparent growth is just the climbing of the stairs to the schoolhouse door. It is with parenthood that the door is opened; it is then the lessons begin.

One result of these lessons of parenthood is wisdom, a deepened perception of human interiors gleaned from the process of watching a baby become a child and a child become an adult. And there is something else gained too. It is what Anne Morrow Lindbergh calls a "timeless inner strength." It is a resilience, usually hidden but nevertheless powerful, the result of having to meet the demands of children day after day, to depend on energy that seems often to have long since vanished, and so to come to discover secret wellsprings of strength that seem to have a source all their own. This inner strength has been traditionally the property of women and Lindbergh contrasts it with the outward, active strength of men; but she rightly says that neither of these are the exclusive property of one sex or the other. Both sexes have increasing opportunities to develop both properties. The clue to the source of her division lies in the fact that women have traditionally been more tightly bound by parenthood than men, and this inner strength is gained through parenthood more surely than any other way.

The response to the spiritual need to nurture, the vision of a world renewed, the development of an inner strength—these then are the elements of a covenant of parenthood. In these the covenant is fulfilled. But before the fulfillment come the struggles. There are demons to be wrestled here also. They are not the same ones met in the desert, but they are no less numerous or less powerful.

The demons of the spirituality of the family, and in fact of community in general, are the frustration, anger, and despair that again and again appear in a life lived primarily for others. It is frustration at the interruptions that inevitably break into every task, the ringing phone, the need to drive across town to pick up a child, the dishes that are no sooner washed than they are dirtied again, the night's sleep shattered by a crying baby. It is anger at a lack of choices, at the feeling that there is nothing else to do but answer others' needs.

The needs of others limit the options of how to spend each day; they also limit the options of a lifetime. Harnessed with a responsibility to care for one or more other people, the number of ways a person might chose to live his or her life grows smaller. Some choices become all but impossible; others are possible but much more difficult than they would be otherwise. Feeling that limitation and that difficulty, it is almost impossible not to feel the anger also.

Worse, however, than either the frustration or the anger is the despair. It is a despair arising from a loss of individuality, a loss of creativity, a loss of a sense of achievement. And, again, because this feeling is naturally most acute in that most intense of all forms of community, the family, it has been most often the province of women. As Lindbergh points out:

[It] is a strange paradox. Woman instinctively wants to give, yet resents giving herself in small pieces. . . . What we fear is not so much that our energy may be leaking away through small outlets as that it may be "going down the drain." . . . Except for the child, woman's creation is so often invisible, especially today. We are working at an arrangement in form, of the myriad disparate details of housework, family routine, and social life. It is a kind of intricate game of cat's-cradle we manipulate on our fingers, with invisible threads. How can one point to this constant tangle of household chores, errands, and fragments of human relations as a creation? It is hard even to think of it as purposeful activity, so much of it is automatic. Woman herself begins to feel like a telephone exchange or a laundromat.[4]

The lack is not one of energy or talent, but of time and of the opportunity to focus time and talent and put them to a specific use. Little by little the energy is doled out, little by little the talent spent. Days pass, and years, and nothing seems to remain. It vanishes into the passing weeks like the wake of a ship, a brief stirring of the waters, then calm. No sign remains of the ship's passing. To feel energy, talent, hopes, and ambitions all being slowly drained, drawn out, and taken away is to know a demon as powerful as any found in the desert.

These are the demons of the spirituality of the family. They must be wrestled just as Antony wrestled those of the desert. And suddenly, unexpectedly, there comes a sense of something more. Even in the midst of the struggle there comes a glimpse into a deeper meaning.

Where the spirituality of life on the edge seeks the face of God, that awesome splendor found only in the presence of the divine, this spirituality offers something else, something subtler, but no less awesome—a recognition of the patterns of eternity. This is probably the oldest of humanity's perceptions of the divine. It was very likely this that those early humans sought to express in their drawings on the walls of caves.

This chapter began with an image of prehistoric man mixing pigments and tracing on the wall of a cave pictures that had been drawn and redrawn for generations. That image grew from an account of recent studies[5] of the cave art of the Cro-Magnons where, with the use of ultraviolet light, it was discovered that Ice Age paintings in a cave in southern France were made up of layer after layer of pigment. The evidence was that they had been drawn and redrawn, and so were perhaps an early record of the human spirit expressing its sense of an eternal rhythm through reenactment and ritual. It is the mysteries at the very center of the family that seek expression in all human rites.

The images prehistoric peoples used most often were seasonal ones, especially those relating to spring. They drew on walls and etched on bones pictures of the animals and plants that appeared at the first thaw—ferns, salmon beginning their run upstream with the ice just breaking from the rivers, the ibix appearing for spring grazing. They lived so close to these things that they could feel the miracle of this rebirth, a miracle that, rather than taking for granted, they valued all the more with each repetition. The earth's seasons represented the eternal. In a community, especially the community of the family, it is the human seasons that come to be known so well, and it is through them that it is possible to discover the eternal.

Having grown from children to adults, a young man and woman each leave their separate homes, find each other, and are married. Then a child is born—a miracle—an incident to them as fresh as if it had never occurred before in human history. But as the child grows the routine takes over. In the repetition of day after day the freshness fades. The baby becomes a child, then a young adult and both she and her parents experience the difficulties that this involves. Then suddenly she is an adult, herself married, and a new spring has come before anyone realized that the old one had passed. And when the new couple bring forth a child, the parents—now grandparents—rediscover the memory of their own spring and find it is not diminished because it has passed but enriched because it has been repeated. In their youth their life had seemed profound because it was unique. Now they see it is not unique, yet it is all the more profound because it touches the eternal. Living human life in the context of the family produces an understanding that discovers in every change the element that never changes.

This truth is the heart of ritual. Rites of the human seasons have come to be called "rites of passage" because they occur at points of change in human life: birth, puberty, marriage, death. But although they mark points of transition, transition itself is not the subject of the ritual, but those elements within the change that do not change. At birth ceremonies the symbolism suggests that this added member is not a break in the unity between husband and wife but renewed evidence of its ties. Rites of puberty and adulthood always in one way or another suggest that the position the boy or girl is now assuming is one he or she was heir to by the fact of birth; now by a second birth—in some cases a birth through baptism, in others a re-enactment of a literal birth, and in still others a birth through knowledge—boys and girls take the place to which they were always entitled. At weddings, where one nuclear family is splintered so another can be formed, the extended family —which has branched apart so often—always gathers to show that despite the breaks, the ties continue. And of course the rites of death all emphasize that although the person is gone something continues. Rituals mark the eternal at times of change.

And it is interesting that the great liturgies meant to mark the incidences in human history when the divine burst through and shattered the rhythm of family life do so with symbols basic to the family—and so by means of the family itself affirm each instance's eternal significance. Passover marks not only exemption from divine wrath, but also the entire period of the exodus and its destruction of a way of life which, although one of slavery, must have had at least some reassuring domestic qualities. The fact that in the desert the bread was not able to rise became symbolic of all the disruption and tragedies, major and minor, that resulted from this abandonment of the life of the home. Now, centuries later, unleavened bread is made a part of a family meal both to recognize the fact of the disruption and to value the power that, despite that disruption, allows the family to endure.

So also the Eucharist. It was over a meal—a Passover meal— that Jesus told his followers, his small family, that their time of sharing together would soon end. At that time he took bread, the one element that by its very commonness and importance to family life symbolized for them as it had for the followers of Moses an eternal presence, and broke it, saying, "This is my body." From that point on he would always be present with them. The most shattering incidence of Christian history became eternal by being drawn into the core of family activity.

This then is the great gift of the spirituality of the family and of the covenant of parenthood in particular—direct participation in the cycles of eternity and the opportunity to see within the processes of individual love the working of a greater Love.

It is a profound understanding, but one never found in visions. Elijah sought God in a great wind, but did not find God there, then in an earthquake, but did not find God there either, then in a fire, but found that, too, empty. He found God at last in a "still, small voice."[6] Like Elijah's, this is a spirituality that finds God in the small incidents of daily life. It hears the "still, small voice" that whispers of a timeless repetition woven into every moment of the life lived to help others grow and learn. This is the voice that the Cro-Magnons heard and that drew them to trace again, as had been traced for generations before, those pictures on the wall of a cave. This is the voice that Mary first heard that night in the stable, and the voice that forms the background of every ritual marking the human seasons. It is the voice every parent knows well—soft, insistent, eternal—it is the voice of a child calling in the night.

3. Separate Spiritualities

Lord, I long to know you as fully as possible. Is that right to ask? I long to know you in the still solitude of my heart; but I long also to know you in the faces and lives of the people of the earth who are your bone and blood. Help me that I never forget one for the other, that I never let the clamor and cries of those around me drown out the words you whisper within, or turn so inward that I no longer notice the clamor of those whose voice is also yours.

The spirituality of the desert and the spirituality of the family are like two parts of a wheel. The first is the rim of the wheel. A life of heights and depths, it is also one that knows the grinding edge. The second is the center of the wheel. Smoother, steadier, closer to that which never changes, it must also experience the frustrations of monotony and of little sense of achievement. If the second has less of the terror and uncertainty of the first, it also has less of its exhilaration. They are two very different ways of life.

The spirituality of life on the edge is an expression of one deeply compelling human need, the need for the transformation that comes of meeting God in God's majesty, in God's awesomeness. It is a craving for the transcendent so single-minded that it comes to consider everything else—even comfort, companionship, and peace of mind—unimportant.

There is a Hindu story of a young man who left home and traveled for many weeks in search of a particular spiritual master whom he at last found sitting in prayer beside a river. He begged the man to take him as his disciple.

"Why should I?" the teacher asked.

"I want to find God," the other answered.

Slowly the master rose to his feet and looked the young man over. "And how badly do you want to find God?" he asked.

The other hesitated, not sure how best to answer. But before he could come up with words that seemed appropriate, the master had grabbed his shoulder and dragged him down the bank and into the river where he held him under the water. Seconds passed, then a minute, then another minute. The young man struggled and kicked, but still the teacher held him down until at last he drew him coughing and gasping out of the water.

"While you were under the water, what was it you wanted?" the teacher asked, when he saw that the other was at last able to speak again.

"Air," the young man said, still panting, "just air."

"And how badly did you want it?"

"All . . . it was all I wanted in the world. With my whole soul I longed only for air."

"Good," said the teacher. "When there comes a time when you long for God in the same way that you have just now longed for air, come back to me and you will become my disciple."

This is the way of life on the edge. A harsh, uncompromising, solitary life, it must willingly accept all God asks in order to know God as God is. The spirituality of life at the center fulfills a very different human need, the need to care for others. By its very nature it is more cautious, more careful, more protective. It seeks a continuity and rhythm at the heart of all that is life-giving, a continuity that shows itself in a daily form as routine, in a communal form as tradition, and in a transcendent form as the Eternal.

Two ways of life, each so different from the other, yet each expressing undeniable spiritual needs. The first allows personal growth, the second the chance to care for others. I believe that there does not exist a single person who does not long for what each way of life has to offer—despite the fact that neither seems the least compatible with the other.

Even in their details the two ways of life vary radically. Life on the edge craves solitude; it cultivates subsistence on the barest of human needs. The life of the family involves the company of others—not merely for the companionship this provides, but as its very reason for existence. And because its object is the care of other people, its hopes are for more than subsistence alone. It asks for enrichment. It does not want to deny food or warmth or comfort, but to give as much as it can of each of these.

And each way of life is suspicious of the other. Judged against the values of the desert, families can seem uncommitted to God or to deeper issues. They seem materialistic, lethargic, caught up in minor details. And yet judged according to the values of the family, life lived on the edge appears unconcerned with human need, irresponsible, and self-absorbed.

Even their goals appear at first glance to be different. One seeks a view of God so powerful that it transforms a person into one who seems set apart from other men and women, a prophet everyone is as afraid to come near as the people of Israel were afraid to approach Moses when he returned from talking with God.[1] The other seeks instead the whispering voice of eternity which only those close to the changes of the human seasons can detect.

Measured by the standards of the spirituality of the family, Antony's entire life in the desert could be called into question by the fact that it could begin only after he had renounced the care of his sister. The girl was left in the care of nuns although the responsibility was his first of all. No more than a child, she had lost both her parents, and now because of his ambition she was to lose him too. With the nuns her needs would be met, but would they love her with the sort of love a family gives? Would they teach her of her past, of her connection to her parents, and them to their parents, and so draw her into the patterns of the community? In this view of things the care of others is the standard against which all things must stand. Antony underwent a life of spiritual growth at his sister's expense. Her care came second to his ambition and so, judged by the values of the family, his accomplishments are suspect.

And yet viewed from the outside, from the vantage of the desert, the weaknesses of these familial values are revealed. The very structures that place such a premium on the care of their members can become the barriers to the movement of the Spirit and of the call of prophesy. Their concern for those within their circle can become a callousness for those outside it, so that the preference for stability which is the hallmark of family life will cause it to tolerate or even encourage injustice, corruption, or the oppression of other groups of people if that seems to make the family more secure. And when the prophet Isaiah commanded, "Enlarge the limits of your home. Spread wide the curtains of your tent,"[2] he was speaking for all the prophets of all ages who, from their position in the desert, see how cruel care can become if it is jealously reserved for a very few.

Two spiritualities, two ways of life, each differing from the other in its goal, intentions, and practical details. Yet different as they are, neither can long continue without the other. They are joined as a flower is joined to the bulb from which it grows. The bulb, misshapen and uninteresting, lies buried a full year in the soil, until from it grows a brilliant flower. In the same way it is always from the community, bland and routine as it seems, that grows the passionate searching of life on the edge. And just as it is through the flower that the bulb is able to reproduce itself, it is through the prophetic spirituality of life on the edge that communities are changed and new ones formed.

Finding a new flower in the garden, one is tempted to cut it and carry it indoors, leaving the uninteresting bulb buried in the ground. Yet without the bulb to nourish it, the flower quickly withers, while the bulb, without the flower, must wait another year to be renewed. Just the same are these two ways of life. Cut off entirely from an intimate human circle, life on the edge withers. And yet if the demands of the group are such that the other life is never allowed to form, then something of great beauty is lost, something that is both its culmination and its means of renewal.

Like a flower and a bulb, a complete spiritual community needs both the prophetic and the nurturing, the spirituality of the desert and that of the family, if it is to grow and to renew itself. But the need exists not only on the communal but also on the individual level. Every soul is both bulb and flower, needing at times to be held and to hold, and at other times to blossom on its own and so be transfigured into its fullest beauty. But since these needs involve ways of life that do not fit easily with each other, there is a powerful temptation to accept one and ignore the other, to sever the flower and bulb in a way that leaves a person either withered,

without the nourishment of love, or else barren, empty and unful-
filled.

The risk is a real one. A person who accepts the life of the desert
relinquishes, as John S. Dunne points out, "the normal joys of
childhood, youth, manhood and age . . . to follow a light as elusive as fire."[3] And in doing this more is lost than the simple plea-
sures of a life with others. Love grows in an atmosphere of love,
and a love that is fed over and over again for a full lifetime of days
has a powerfully sustaining warmth which—soft and gentle—is
easily passed over unnoticed, although it is this more than anything
else that draws a person to his or her full humanity. Only with
difficulty do people adjust themselves to the colder air apart from
love. But those who live too long the life on the edge can become
so accustomed to this cold that the warmth of human love is no
longer something with which they are comfortable.

In his lifetime Thomas Merton reached out to millions with his
books. But the more people discovered his writings, the more he
seemed to be drawn to deeper solitude. He became not only a
monk, but a hermit, retiring to a secluded cottage on the monastery grounds. In the year or so just before his death, Merton's
friends began to feel uneasy when they visited him. He seemed
distant, beyond their reach. "No matter how much you talked,"
one said, "you got the feeling that he was always apart."[4] Two of
his oldest friends, Edward Rice and Robert Lax, found themselves
sharing their impressions when they met. As Rice remembers, "I
told Lax that I thought the Old Boy (which was what we called him)
wasn't relating to people; Lax agreed. Now, I wonder if he was not
literally in another world."[5] One of the greatest dangers of life on
the edge is how quickly being in another world can become simply
not relating to people.

For the spirituality of the family the danger is a loss of another
sort. It is the loss of creativity, the loss of opportunity, the loss of
a sense of purpose that comes from ignoring too long hopes and
talents not quite like those of anyone else. It is the loss that comes
of stifling that longing that—tugging and pulling—seeks to draw a
person into the presence of God. It is the emptiness that comes of

setting aside the urge to become all that it is possible to become in order to attend to the many details essential to the working of a family.

Each way of life has precisely what the other lacks and lacks what the other gives. Both express powerful needs that both the human soul and the human community have no choice but to try to fulfill. And yet only with difficulty are they joined. And in the history of spirit the union has been attempted in many different ways.

In the Roman Catholic church, especially before Vatican II, the spirituality of the desert was reserved for priests and religious and that of the family for the laity. It was thought enough that the two were joined in one church. There was no hope or need that they might ever be joined within one individual.

The Jewish answer, as found in the structure of the eighteenth-century *shtetls* of eastern Europe, was for the two ways of life to be divided between husband and wife. The husband spent his time in study and prayer while the wife provided for the family. The husband's life was centered in Hasidic mysticism or study of the Talmud, the wife's in care. In the Jewish response the two ways of life were brought together in one family, but again, not in one individual.

In Indian culture the problem is approached another way. A Hindu male sees his life as divided ideally into four parts: student, householder, hermit, and ascetic. During the first two of these stages he lives the spirituality of the family, first studying, then marrying and having children. It is then he fulfills his need to nurture. When his children have grown, he begins the spirituality of life on the edge, first by seeking solitude, then by practicing self-denial and concentrating his energy on his search for God. Here, for men at least, the two spiritualities are brought together in one life—though relegated to different periods of that life. To get them both in, however, a person must live the full span of a normal lifetime—or else believe as the Hindus do that there are many different lifetimes, so that a person cut short from achieving all four stages in one could hope to do better in the next.

A fourth possibility is that offered by St. Benedict in the *Rule of St. Benedict* and by others who have attempted to build communities of men or of women where seclusion and active involvement with others are interwoven in a routine that includes both solitary prayer and communal worship and work. For over fifteen hundred years this has been one of the most successful and enduring attempts to blend the two ways of life. But here too the restrictions of the community are tight enough that the more prophetic and visionary aspects of life on the edge become severely limited. And although in the Middle Ages many monasteries and convents became havens for unwanted or orphaned children, the need for quiet and order makes it a difficult place to adapt to life with children.

The fact is that although there have been attempts such as these to try to draw both ways of life into one community, there seems never to have been in the long chronicle of religious history any attempt to approach in a systematic way the possibility that one person might actually be able to experience the benefits of *both* the spirituality of life on the edge and that of life at the center. The lucky few were at least offered a choice between the two. Most simply took whichever one life decreed for them.

Probably only recently have men and women had a chance to even hope for both. It is an opportunity never before offered. But those attempting to give expression to both ways of life are discovering how difficult this is to accomplish. Anyone who has tried knows what it means. It means that the days spent in whatever is involved in self-development—creative projects, career, retreats—must always be at the expense of the family. Arrangements have to be made, babysitters called, schedules adjusted, until finally there it is, a little block of time for creativity and self-development. But soon it is clear that something has suffered. Children have been put to one side, the marriage has not been tended, small rifts and wounds have appeared because the love that holds the family together has not been cared for as it should.

Then efforts shift. Time is spent with children, more care goes into the preparation of meals, there are outings, and husband and wife arrange dinners alone together. But soon again evidence grows that something else is being lost. Restlessness and uneasiness begin to creep in, a stirring again of that longing for self-expression, for time alone, for contact with those deeper mysteries uncluttered by human details. Eventually the longing becomes unbearable and arrangements are shifted again.

Life lived this way feels awkward, unsteady. It seems to be always off balance. But our task is to find ways to steady that balance—or else learn to live with the imbalance and so transform its stumbling steps into a lifetime dance that draws into one experience two ways of life, that lived among people and that lived alone in the desert, seeking to know both the human and the divine.

This must be one of the goals, but we will have to postpone its consideration for a time. Before a balance can be attempted between the life on the edge and that of the center, this second way of life must be more carefully examined. The special spiritual gifts of the life of the family have never been fully appreciated. For too long the spirituality of the family has been either not recognized at all or else regarded as something distinctly inferior to other spiritual disciplines. Christianity continues to live in the shadow of an ideal that views the life of solitary self-dedication as its supreme expression. Catholics and Protestants alike remain in the shadow of the monastery.

This is more obvious perhaps within the Catholic Church. The widespread delusion among the clergy that the Church is effectively promoting a view of the spiritual potential of the family is possible only because of what amounts to a conspiracy of silence among the laity. The opinions and complaints that are an inevitable part of any discussion where Catholic parishioners are gathered to talk among themselves are instantly suppressed whenever they are joined by a priest. These discussions always include a strong undercurrent of bitterness that the Church's words seem to support families while their actions do not. The fact that a calling to serve God as a priest must also mean a calling to be celebate; the fact that women can in no circumstance be ordained, something which, despite the arguments usually given, seems to be most closely related to some obscure notion of women as unqualified because they have traditionally been more closely associated with the family than have men—these show the Church's true feelings. It is the relationship with the family (and women seem to be seen as permanently related to family, regardless of their status) that, more than anything else, bars a person from serving God through ordination. Even the fact that priests are moved so freely from parish to parish with no parishioner involvement in such a decision reveals that this relationship which has often been compared with marriage—the marriage of a priest with his people—is one that the Church does not hesitate to dissolve into divorce, preferring to promote the separateness and solitariness of its priests over the care and continuity of the parish. No Catholic layperson is fooled by the occasional homily in praise of the family; the Church neither recognizes nor values the real gifts of the spirituality of family life. And, unquestionably, they are seen as incompatible with the spirituality of the edge which the Church encourages for its priests.

But this problem is far from being one exclusive to Catholics. Christianity as a whole has still much to learn of the unique spiritual qualities of family life, and Protestants suffer from this lack as much as any. A woman, herself Protestant, told me of her reaction when she first realized how little Christianity appreciated the family. She was taking time out from a career as a lawyer to take care of her two small children. During her first pregnancy she had feared that she would feel lost and aimless once her main job became the care of a child. Instead, she found herself enjoying her role as a parent more than she ever dreamed she would. Something unexpected began to bother her, though. As weeks and months passed her irritation mounted, until finally she could take it no longer. She made an appointment to see her minister. After he had greeted her and she had sat down in the chair opposite him, she suddenly blurted out:

"I'm finished. I'm never going to read the New Testament again."

The minister stared at her, stunned. The woman was among the most dedicated in his congregation. This was the last thing he had expected to hear from her.

"I don't understand," he said. "Why not?"

"Because Jesus does not seem to have a single good thing to say about families. He says that a person who follows him must leave his wife, children, and parents. He says that this person must also give away all he owns—can I really raise my children like that? And what of Mary and Martha? It's Mary who spends her time adoring Christ, rather than Martha who works to keep him fed, who Jesus says has the better part. Where do I fit in?"

She was right to feel upset. It is not Jesus' words themselves that are the problem, but how they have been interpreted over the years. Too often they have been used to encourage and promote dramatic imitations of some of the external expressions of Jesus' life, at the expense of the very truth he lived—the truth of God's love for each of us and of our need to express that love in our love for others. The time has now come when the truly spiritual gifts of family life must be discovered for all that they are, something that draws people closer to the eternal while transforming and molding them into those who can know and give God's love in a way in which nothing else is capable. It is also time to find ways in which this spirituality of life at the center can be connected to that of life on the edge—not because it is inferior to it, but because in the end most people seem to crave some part of both for complete fulfillment. Either life lived exclusive of the other—only on the edge or only at the center—risks leaving people with a sense of something incomplete, a part of themselves as yet unformed.

And so now that both ways of life have been characterized and their apparent incompatibility noted, we can go forward in the second part of this book by going backward; we return once more to the life of the family, the life at the center, in order to draw from it the full account of its treasures, the complete story of its secret wisdom and its mysteries, and so find all that it has to offer to those who have adopted the rigors of its discipline as their own. From there we will proceed to something that for most of human history has been thought impossible: ways in which a person can learn from both ways of life and live both on the edge and at the center.

II. THE FAMILY AS A SPIRITUAL DISCIPLINE

4. Two Stories

God, bless those whose lives bless our lives, whose love for us has been the seed from which our love for others grew. Help us to appreciate them. They are so close to you that they have come to express your goodness in even the smallest of daily acts, but are so close to us that we may no longer even notice.

A life lived at the center is one seldom seen by any except those closest to it. Its story is rarely told. And yet there is great drama involved in a life of care for others; those who are able to live it fully, meeting its struggles with strength and courage, are heroic figures capable of reaching those they will never see, forming as they do a love that ripples through generations. Here are the stories of two lives that have touched me in this way. The first is of a man known by all my family as Grandfather. I called him Grandfather too, although in the actual sequence of things he was my great-grandfather.

For twenty years he strode through the rooms of my childhood and youth, this great-grandfather of mine, wearing even in summer a heavy, dark suit and in winter a great horsehair coat which, when slipped off, revealed a frame small, thin, almost fragile, yet infused with a strange power. Even as a small child I sensed it, so that when he crouched to my level and said in a tone of exaggerated wonder, "My, my. Just look at this boy. How big he is getting!" I would bury my face in my mother's skirt. It was not that I feared him—not him of all people—but before him I felt something like awe.

There was a special quality to him—mysterious, bright, and strong. He spoke often to God and that intrigued me. I had heard about God in Sunday school. I knew the stories of how God sent a flood to kill all the people of the earth but helped Noah build an ark, sparing him and his family; how God parted the waters of the

Dead Sea for Moses and the Israelites, then closed them again over the army of the Pharaoh; how God hounded peaceful men to prophesy his words, putting them in great peril. And I knew also how, most puzzling of all, God sent his son to be killed so that he could be raised from the dead. But in these stories God seemed distant, menacing, very different from how Grandfather spoke of God. Grandfather spoke of God as of someone present right there in the room, listening and responding to all that was said, and yet somehow also touching all the rest of the universe, an intimate—yet infinite—presence. God was gentle, small, human. God was vast, mysterious, powerful. God was both eternal Lord of the universe and closest of friends.

As a young man Grandfather had had to leave the farm where he was raised to find work in the city mills to support the family. For twenty years he worked among the dirt and smoke and pounding machinery, supporting his mother and father and, later, his own wife and family.

In a photograph taken on the day of their wedding, Grandfather sits while his bride stands beside him, her hand resting lightly on his shoulder. Even the formality of the pose cannot hide that extraordinary quality each brought to it and the obvious love they shared. He looks bright, happy, and so very young, and she—slender and beautiful—seems no less a child than he; but her glance has a quality that differs from his look of complete innocence in a hint of unwavering confidence. In the years to come her confidence would grow, just as in a strange way his innocence would too, and in later life her complete self-certainty would be balanced by his complete openness. All his life he never referred to her in any way other than "my wonderful Susie."

Their life was uncertain and hard. The youngest of their three children died of fever. Whenever there were lay-offs at the mills, Grandfather would have to move his small family back to the country to pick up farm work; but always he returned with them to the city, as if attracted by something he saw in the lives of those who lived there.

At thirty-eight this man who had never had more than three years of formal schooling was asked to found a mission church in the district where he worked. This he did. For the next sixty years he preached four sermons a week to those who came—to the poor, to the despairing, to the drunks who stumbled in from the street, and to the growing numbers of a regular congregation.

His sermons were always exactly an hour long and moved with an energy all their own. It was never the words themselves, but something behind the words that drew in those who listened. It was as if there was a voice speaking behind his voice, pulling all who heard it closer, closer, until, as tension mounted both in him and in the congregation, it would rise to a sudden crescendo and he would close his eyes and cry out, "Praise the Lord, praise the Lord," answered with cries of "Amen" by those around him.

And yet what was most compelling about Grandfather was not this public presence but a capacity to truly care for others such as I have rarely found since. He deeply loved his wife and children and expressed his love, but more, he had an extraordinary ability to give a person total attention, total acceptance. As a child I would go to him in a crowd as he stood talking to one or two others, tug on his coat, and say, "Grandfather, Grandfather." He would finish his sentence, then turn to me, stoop down to my level, ask me what I wanted, and wait for me to tell him. And as he waited he looked at me with eyes that told me that I need not hurry, that there was time; eyes that said that I need not fear what he would think of what I might say, anything would be fine; eyes that seemed to see the person I most truly was and accept that person. His was a caring of the deepest sort. People were drawn to him because he seemed able to calmly recognize and accept what not even they could accept in themselves.

His wife, Susie, died when she was seventy-eight and he eighty-five. From that day onward he could never mention anything about her or the life they shared together without beginning to weep silently as he talked.

Whenever the family gathered he would pray. It would come as we parted. He would rise, but only to stretch his legs because immediately after that he would kneel, his elbows resting on the chair where he had just been sitting, his head held in his cupped palms. Then everyone else would kneel too, we children with the rest, and he would begin his prayer. They were long prayers. He would thank God for bringing us together. He would name each person in the room and thank the Lord for them individually. Then he would remember those not there and pray for their safety and health. Finally he would continue, "And we want to remember, too, Lord, those who have gone before us." Here his voice would begin to waver. "Yes, we want to remember them, for we miss them so." By now he was weeping openly, but he would continue. "We miss them with all our heart, Lord, but we know they are with you and we long to be reunited with them again in your presence." And here he would become suddenly jubilant. "We look forward, Lord, to that time when we will be together again with our dear ones in your kingdom. What a day that will be, Lord! What a glorious day that will be! Amen."

A man of openness, humor, and warmth, Grandfather fascinated me. And yet there came a time when, as a teenager, I began to believe that I had outgrown a faith in God like his. Grandfather had a special inner strength and a magnificent capacity for love. I could see that. He believed that qualities such as these came from God. This I doubted. I had come to consider God as a vague, impersonal force, something that, if it existed at all, could never really touch me. To me the intimate, personal God Grandfather knew was no more than a delusion.

Grandfather was in his late nineties when I left for college. He still preached several times a week—preaching his last sermon on his ninety-ninth birthday—but I avoided these. And I had come to dread the prayer that inevitably marked our parting. My life was, I felt, worlds away from his. I felt nothing but embarrassment when I knelt beside my chair as he, kneeling beside his, prayed his long, emotional prayers, always breaking into tears, always with phrase and manner hopelessly out of date.

One afternoon in late November I took time off from college to visit him. He was living with his daughter then. It was she who met me at the door.

"He's not been well," she said in response to my question. "He has an infection in his leg. It's not bad, but his circulation is now so poor that it doesn't heal. He grows weaker every day."

She paused. "And you know," she began slowly, as if describing something she knew I would never believe of him, "he sometimes even has trouble walking across the room."

She took me to his bedroom. He sat on the edge of the bed fully dressed. He smiled when I came in and waved, but he did not get up as he had always done in the past. I pulled a chair near to him.

"My, my," he said, looking me over slowly. For a moment I expected him to continue, as he always had when I was a child, "Just look at this boy. How big he is getting!" Instead, he smiled slyly, as if aware of what I expected, and kept silent.

A Bible was open on his lap, an unpleasant reminder of the prayer that would inevitably be the final ordeal of our meeting. He marked his place, closed the book, and laid it beside him, then began to question me about my life. I answered as vaguely as possible. The world in which I lived seemed too far removed from his. I was sure he would never understand it. Then too, at that moment, I felt suddenly uneasy that he might somehow discover that I had fully rejected the faith in God upon which his life had been built. And because I felt uncomfortable with what I was saying, I talked all the longer, trying to make my words sound plausible to him and to myself.

He listened in silence, his eyes half closed, his head turned to one side. Several times he nodded slowly.

When I finished, he was silent a moment; then he reached under his pillow and took out a harmonica. He asked me if I had any favorite songs. Caught off guard—this particular talent of his had been entirely unknown to me—I could not think of a single title that he would have had any chance of knowing, so he struck up some of his own favorites. None of the tunes I recognized, but as he finished each one he paused to tell me its name—old love songs, every one.

He played until he was out of breath, at least twenty minutes. By then his daughter had opened the door and motioned to me that it was time for his nap. I stood and told him I had to go.

This time he pulled himself to his feet and braced himself on the headboard of the bed. Grimly I awaited what would follow. Once he lowered himself into a kneeling position, I would have to kneel too, and in that humiliating posture endure the long prayer I had been dreading.

But he did not kneel. Instead he took my hand in both of his, shook it, then drew me closer and kissed me on the cheek.

It was several moments before he let my hand drop. When at last he did, I said good-bye and went to the door, but just before I opened it he called to me.

"When you pray," he said, "if you pray, remember me."

I nodded. He smiled. In my last glimpse of him before closing the door he was sitting on the bed once more, waving.

Those were his last words to me. I had underestimated the depth of his love, the fullness of his ability to recognize and to accept in me even my rejection of the faith he knew to be the center of life.

One week later he got out of bed during one of the afternoon napping periods insisted on by his daughter. He hated napping and was always thinking of reasons to get up. This time his excuse was one he had never used before.

"What is it, Father?" his daughter asked, as he came into the room.

"As I was lying in bed just now," he said, "an angel came to me. The angel said, 'Come on, Will. It's time to go.' I told him I was ready, but asked if I could say good-bye to you before I went. He agreed and said he'd be back in half an hour."

She sighed.

"Father, you know that you should be napping now."

"I just wanted to say good-bye and that I love you very much."

"I love you too, Father."

"Thank you for taking care of me these past years. I'll see you soon."

"Of course you will. Now, try to get some rest before dinner."

He kissed her and returned to his room. Forty-five minutes later she felt suddenly uneasy as she passed his closed door. She opened it a crack and peered inside. He lay on his bed with his eyes closed. She opened the door further and approached the bed. He was dead. He had died two weeks short of his hundredth birthday.

Grandfather's life was a miracle of life lived at the center. In his ability to be present to those around him he was always present to God. And because he saw God in every person he met, he helped others to see God in themselves. No words could have done it: only a look, a smile, a pause with full attention. He changed many lives without ever opening his mouth.

Another story of a life lived at the center is of a woman named Sarah. The youngest of a family of eight children, Sarah was the only one to be born in America after her parents emigrated from Italy to a small mining town in central Pennsylvania. Whenever she asked when her birthday was, her father would say only, "You were born when the flowers bloomed." The year at least she knew; it was 1906.

Her father worked in the mine. He left as the sun rose, his lunch bucket in his hand, and returned as the sun set, his face and clothes blackened with coal dust. During that time, while above the long westward shadows of early morning shrank smaller and smaller, all but vanished at noon, then slowly began their long reach toward the east, his only light was what he kept mounted on his helmet, pointed at the hard blocks of earth he spent his days chipping away at little by little with his pick, working deeper and deeper.

Her mother had a boarding house, letting rooms and cooking meals for the men, miners all, who stayed there. She would be up before daybreak to prepare breakfast before beginning her chores of cooking, washing, and baking bread in a great, outdoor oven.

Sarah helped her mother. She bent over the washing tubs, scrubbing out the heavy coal dust by rubbing shirts and pants back and forth over the washboards. She made the beds, fried the meat for dinner, and kneaded dough and formed it into loaves to be carried to the outdoor oven.

And sometimes she would slip away to meet her friends and run in the fields or play in the creek below the suspension bridge which cut the town in half.

The town was small—about two hundred families. The mine was what kept the place alive. Every child there quickly learned to fear one sound above all others, the emergency whistle that signaled a cave-in. It blew many times as Sarah was growing up; she with the others would rush to the mine to wait for news of her father and, once they became teenagers, of her brothers. Men from other tunnels would emerge to help with the digging out, but there were always those who did not return, or else were carried crushed or suffocated to the surface, whitened eyes staring vacantly from darkened faces. Her father and brothers always survived, where fathers and brothers of friends sometimes did not.

At eighteen Sarah married. She only met her husband three times before their wedding. To her the man was all but a stranger; he had just arrived from Italy the year before. But since he came from the same village as Sarah's family, her parents knew him, or at least they knew his family, which was just as good. Her father had known his father, her mother, his mother. They were good people. That was enough. The son and the daughter were married.

Sarah moved with her husband to a strange new life in the city. He set up a barber shop and his family soon came from Italy to join them. Soon a son was born, then a daughter, then a second son. It was while still a toddler that her third child was diagnosed as having muscular dystrophy. The doctor told Sarah that the boy would not live to his fifth birthday.

Muscular dystrophy is a crippling disease. Little by little it robs those it strikes of muscular coordination, control of speech, and eventually of the ability to move about and care for themselves. The disease progressed, then lapsed for a time, then progressed in the child.

The Great Depression had struck and the barber shop was not

doing well, but now there was medicine to buy in addition to the other things needed for a family of five. Sarah began to take in laundry and when she found that that was not enough, she began to work at other part-time jobs—house cleaning, cooking in a high-school cafeteria. She also began baking bread, dozens of loaves at a time. After school her daughter would load the still warm bread onto a small wagon to sell to stores and families in the neighborhood.

And always Sarah cared for her children. Already her son was requiring special care. It was at this time that she began going to daily Mass at six in the morning to pray for help for her son and strength for herself. The boy's fifth birthday came, the one he was not expected to live to see, then his sixth, then his seventh. The disease was progressing much slower than the doctor expected it would, but still it continued.

In desperation Sarah wrote to President Roosevelt. Knowing that he too had suffered a crippling disease, she hoped he might be able to help her son. A few weeks after she wrote she received a letter from the White House. A presidential aide had written to say that arrangements had been made for the boy to be cared for at a major clinic in Maryland. Sarah took the boy for his initial examination but had deep doubts. The care was supposed to be good, but the child would be so far away.

The doctor examined the boy, looked over his records, then took Sarah into his office.

"What I've seen is a miracle," he said. "There is no medical explanation for your son living as long as he has. We can give him no better care than you have given him, and there is something special that only you can give—your love. That's what has sustained him so long. I suggest you continue just as you are doing."

Her son was fourteen when he died. On the day of the funeral her husband returned, took to bed, and did not leave it until he too died six months later.

Now, support for herself and her two teenage children was entirely hers. While continuing to work at her other jobs and caring for her family, she began to go to beauty school in the evenings, learning hairdressing and eventually turning the small barber shop her husband had had in the front room of the house into a beauty shop.

In the long years of her son's illness, Sarah had spent much time with him in the children's wards of hospitals. There she met many others like her son and met the mothers who, like herself, spent every hour they were allowed with their children. But she also met children no one cared enough to visit, children who had been abandoned, orphaned, or who came from homes where the need was so desperate that no one even had the time for visits. In the midst of her own grief she felt the special grief revealed in the faces of these small children who lay on their hospital beds and watched with large silent eyes as day after day people came to talk and play with the other children in the ward, while they remained alone, unloved. Even then, she began stopping to talk with one or two, after being with her son. And if she brought some special little treat for him, she would bring along something for them too.

After her son died, even the memory of those children's wards was painful, but still the thought of those children haunted her so much that she knew that eventually she would have to go back. She did. Once more she climbed the stairs she had climbed so often before. Again she walked past the rows of beds she had passed so often, and past the bed, now occupied by another, where her son had lain. Several of the children she used to stop and see were still there. She began again her daily visits to these and to others who had no one to talk to. This continued for several months, until one day the head nurse, who had recently been asking questions about her and watching whenever she came and went, came up to her.

"You should not be here," she said.

"But this is visiting time, and I'm here visiting these children."

"Only relatives of patients are permitted to visit."

"These are children no one visits. They cannot be left alone this way."

"That doesn't matter. The rules say only relatives of patients may visit. And besides, those children aren't used to that kind of attention. What happens if they get better and leave here? You can't adopt them. Now, I'm going to have to ask you to leave."

Sarah left the hospital and found a quiet park bench. Her grief now seemed total. She wept, crying for her son, her husband, her family, herself, and for those children she would not see again. When the tears subsided, she picked up her purse and stood. Just then something occurred to her. She could not adopt those particular children, she knew that, but perhaps there were others who needed her care. It was soon afterward that she applied to become a foster parent and for many years following, years that stretched long after the time when her own children had left home and married, she had girls in their early teens come to live with her. Some stayed a few weeks; others stayed for years.

And so began a pattern that would be hers for decades to follow. She rose at five in the morning, then walked to church for six o'clock Mass; she returned to make breakfast for those she cared for, meet her appointments for permanents or hairdos, make a quick lunch, and finally cook dinner. And not a day went by when she did not bake bread. She fit it in between her appointments and later on in the evening. She baked dozens of loaves at a time. Companies that sold to bakeries now regularly delivered one-hundred-pound sacks of flour to her door. But the time had long passed since she baked her bread for sale. Every loaf she made was given away. She baked for churches trying to raise money; she baked for soup kitchens serving food to the poor and homeless; she baked for her family and for the growing numbers of grandchildren; she baked for any of her neighbors who she felt needed extra care or for anyone else she heard of who needed help.

Her philosophy was simple and direct. "God tells us to give what we have," she would say. "All I have to give is my bread."

But she was giving much more than that. She was giving a special kind of love, a love that at once reached out to others while also making her life all of one piece, so that everything she did, routine or ordinary as it might otherwise seem, came to express that love. It was there as she walked to church every morning. It was there in the care and sympathy with which she listened to her customers who remained steadfastly loyal to her; it was clear that they received from her much more than care for their hair. It was there in the way she would laugh with and listen to the girls who stayed with her and the grandchildren who were always visiting. It was there in how she made bread.

"Watch how you knead it," she would tell her granddaughters as they huddled around her. "Let it rise and then punch it down." She would lean over the great ball of dough, working it with all her strength. Then she would form it into loaf after loaf, glaze each with egg white, sprinkle with sesame seed, then place the trays on the racks of her two ovens, watching carefully until the crust turned just the right shade of brown before removing them to cool as the next batch went in. And as the bread cooled she would run her hand lightly along the top of several of the loaves as if to make sure that they were just right, finally patting one gently —the sign that everything was just as it should be. Several hours of nearly every day of the week she spent making bread. But each time she did, the work received her total attention.

And after nearly forty years of this, there came an afternoon when one of her granddaughters, the youngest, who was just graduating from college, called her on the phone.

"Gram, I want to go to Mass this afternoon and I want you to go with me."

"Of course I'll go, but—wait a minute, what is today?—I don't think that there is a Mass this afternoon."

"There is. I already checked. Please come."

"Well, all right."

"I'll meet you at your house and we can walk."

Sarah was walking more slowly these days and leaned on her granddaughter's arm. As they approached the church, she saw her son, her son's wife, her daughter, and her daughter's husband all standing on the church steps.

"What are they doing here?" Sarah asked.

"I guess they want to go to church too," her granddaughter answered.

But they were waiting there for her and, as she reached the steps, her son and daughter each took an arm.

Inside, the church was filled with people, but as she entered they all began to clap. She stopped and looked around. Every person there was someone she knew, someone she had helped. The whole church was filled with people she had touched. Many she had not seen for years. Most had traveled great distances, hundreds or even thousands of miles to be there that day. Slowly she walked down the aisle, wiping away the tears as person after person came forward to take her hand, to hug her, to kiss her. Here were brothers, now long retired, there cousins with whom she had played as a girl, over there were neighbors she had helped so often over the years. Among the crowd she saw the faces of the girls who had lived with her as her foster children, now married, with careers and with children of their own. She saw her grandchildren with their wives and husbands, whose children, her great-grand-children, were staring at her over the tops of the pews. Every-where she turned were friends and relatives, all of whom had felt her special love.

Her son and daughter were still beside her and guided her to the front pew where she was to sit during this special Mass in her honor. But just as she reached it, the youngest of her great-grand-children, a girl of two, came up to her with a bouquet of roses.

"Here, Great-grandma," she said. "These are yours."

Sarah took them, paused for a moment, then, carrying the flow-ers carefully in her arms, slowly approached the front of the church. There on a table stood a statue of another mother holding a child in her arms. On that table Sarah lay the roses.

"Here," she said softly. "These are yours."

5. The Practice of the Presence of God

Lord, you are with me. Your love is even now a part of my life. Your truth was given life in history; your truth is the hope that is to come. But neither one nor the other of these has meaning apart from the truth of your presence here and now. Draw me into that presence. Help me to feel how near you are, the breath of my breath, the life of my life.

These two lives speak of something intangible. It is not what either person did that was so significant—not Grandfather's preaching or his meeting with people, not Sarah's care for her family or for those in need or her baking of bread—but a special quality they both brought to these activities and to everything else they did, that made these two people so extraordinary. All that they did became an expression of God's presence in their lives.

This is a truth Christians have long known but too seldom made a reality within their own lives. Paul knew its importance. Several times in his letters he refers to the kingdom of God as something Christians must experience as both "already" and as "not yet"— that is, as both here now and still to come. Most often he talks of this in terms of death and resurrection.

For if we have been united with [Christ] in a death like his, we shall certainly be united with him in a resurrection like his. We know that our old self was crucified with him so that the sinful body might be destroyed, and we might no longer be enslaved to sin. For he who has died is freed from sin. But *if we have* died with Christ, we believe that *we shall* also live with him. For we know that Christ being raised from the dead will never die again; death no longer has dominion over him. The death he died he died to sin, once for all, but the life he lives he lives to God. *So also you must consider yourselves dead to sin and alive to God in Christ Jesus.*[1]

The death of which Paul speaks is one that dies to an old life in order to rise into a new one that lives in the full reality of God's presence, into a life so powerfully alive that death has no hold on it. It is resurrection from a dull, deadened existence into one fully alive to God.

All Christians await a better time. They await the fulfillment that Jesus called the kingdom of God; they are painfully aware that there is much that is incomplete, much that is "not yet." Things are very far from right. There is great sorrow and suffering. There is injustice, misery, cruelty, blind hatred, destruction, and fear. These exist for all to see. But for Christians each of these is also a reminder that ahead of them is God's kingdom, something for which they can pray, hope, and work. And yet as true as it is that both we and the world as a whole are imperfect and incomplete, it is also true that both we and it are just exactly as we should be— that the kingdom of God is here already. Saying this does not involve hiding from trouble and pain or pretending that they do not exist. It involves, instead, one extraordinary discovery—that we, those very beings who know this trouble and feel this pain, are also creatures formed by God, beings in whom God lives.

But we have this treasure in earthen vessels, to show that the transcendent power belongs to God and not to us. We are afflicted in every way, but not crushed; perplexed, but not driven to despair; persecuted, but not forsaken; struck down, but not destroyed; always carrying in the body the death of Jesus, so that the life of Jesus may also be manifested in our bodies. For while we live we are always being given up to death for Jesus' sake, so that the life of Jesus may be manifested in our mortal flesh. So death is at work in us, but life in you.[2]

This is the discovery, as Paul says in Ephesians, "that you, being rooted and grounded in love, may have the power to comprehend with all the saints what is the breadth and length and height and depth, and to know the love of Christ which surpasses knowledge, that you may be filled with all the fullness of God."[3]

Together these form the Christian reality—the "already," which is the fullness of the presence of God now at hand, and the "not yet," for which we wait in expectant, impatient hope. What we have and what we hope for, each is half of a total reality meant to be held together, but one too often splintered in preference for a preoccupation with the "not yet," the expectation of what is to come. The tendency has always been strong in Christianity to look toward a coming apocalypse, a better life in heaven, or a new and better society while ignoring the fact that God's reality is with us already, that the kingdom of God is here now. Christianity is the story of something that happened in the past that points to a better future through a life with God in the present. But too often the emphasis is placed on Christianity's past truth and its future hope and it is forgotten that the present is the key. Unless we are able to live the reality of God's presence here and now, Christianity's past becomes meaningless and its future impossible. But discover the reality of God fully present, and the truth of Christianity's past becomes indubitable, its future inevitable.

But this split between "already" and "not yet" is the very one seen earlier between life lived at the center and life lived on the edge. Life lived at the edge seeks to imitate the rigors of Jesus' own life, to follow him in his loneliness, in his hunger, in his struggle and pain. It seeks to know him by knowing his life. It is also prophetic. It speaks out in the face of human incompleteness and injustice. It points out our need to reconcile ourselves with each other and with God. It lives the "not yet."

Life at the center lives the reality of the presence of God in the now of every moment of every act that is done. It is a life that sees the greatness of the smallest of tasks, since these, as all others, are of God's work. Life lived at the center is an expression of God's immediate presence. It is not a life of imitation; nor one of anticipation; it is instead a life of participation, participation in the truth of its own full reality. But in saying this, no one should think that life at the center seeks some special mode of existence, some level of being somehow above the mundane toil of the day to day. Just the opposite—it is life at its most human. It is not a life that ignores or avoids the ordinary, but one that lives it fully, since it knows that in so doing it expresses the profoundest of the profound. It is a life that may know pain and trouble; it certainly knows routine. It lives this as it lives everything—moment to moment—and in so doing touches the eternal.

It is a way of life that lives great truths in every act, truths that are recognized by no one at the time, least of all by those who express them, but may be seen years later for what they are by those whose lives they altered. When Grandfather interrupted a conversation to listen to a little boy tugging at his coat, turning to him with eyes that made that boy their whole world, inviting him to take all the time he needed and to say whatever he wanted—when Grandfather did this it never occurred to him that it might be anything but the most ordinary of acts. And he was right. It was ordinary, especially for him, since it was entirely consistent with the love that was his life. It was a small thing, done with complete spontaneity. But being that boy who had tugged at his coat and met his eyes, I know that, as ordinary as it was, it was also profound. Over twenty-five years have passed since that moment came and went unnoticed by anyone else, and yet I can still feel what it was like to have been held in the full acceptance of those eyes. And it was simply *because* there was nothing extraordinary for him in what he did, consistent as it was with everything else, that it was extraordinary for me. It is because he lived so fully the truth of each small act that his life touched so many so deeply.

And the same is true of Sarah. To live a life such as hers with more than its share of difficulty, pain, and loss, and yet not let the hardships and struggle cause her to close herself to love and retreat into bitterness and suspicion, as they might have done for others, but open her instead, so that she cared for many more people than she would ever have needed to—it is this that made her someone symbolizing love and courage to so many. Her difficulties in caring for her family after her husband's death did not close her off into her own world; they made her more finely attuned to other's hardships. Her sorrows revealed to her the sorrows of others. Her response to the pain of loss was to ease the pain of others. And when these gifts of courage and of love, expressed in all she did, were expressed also in the baking of bread, those who watched came to have a sense of the true art of living. So full is her attention to this process, which is for her at once so special and so routine, a simple act that somehow expresses all that it means to care for others; that her granddaughters, my wife, Pamela, and the others, who grew up watching her bake, often say that they cannot themselves bake bread without a powerful sense that Sarah is in the room with them.

This is the heart of Christianity. It must have been this ability to love openly without fear and to live fully all that was occurring in each moment that first attracted people to Jesus. Long before most people had any sense of who Jesus was, there were crowds gathering around him. According to the Gospel of Mark, even Jesus' disciples were confused as to who he was until the very end. And it was not the miracles alone that attracted them, because Jesus had followers even before he worked a single wonder. What drew people to him could not have been what they knew about him or even the works they saw him perform. It was something else. It was some quality, some way of standing, some way of looking at them, of speaking to them that revealed a love and acceptance for each of them that was greater than the love and acceptance they felt they deserved. Jesus expressed through his life how present God was in each of their lives—infinitely more present than they ever could have hoped. Jesus proclaimed the "already" of the Christian message and continued to proclaim it even while, nailed to the cross, he also proclaimed the "not yet."

Together they state the Christian truth—"already" and "not yet"—God is fully present, God has still more to give. But of the two it is the "already" that Christians most often forget or else remain content to state in words, never seeking to discover its full meaning in their lives. And yet this "already" can never be known through simple words which can only form an idea in the mind— it must be felt. It must be lived so fully day to day that it becomes like breathing, so much a part of life that it is hardly noticed. The "already" is only half of the total Christian truth, but it is upon it that the realization of both depends. Until women and men come to discover the truth of God's presence in their lives, and discover it not merely as some statement they affirm or deny but as a living reality, they will never recognize the fullfillment of the "not yet," the fulfillment of God's total gift.

So great a truth, it is seldom realized quickly. Only slowly does it become something more than a pious statement, "God is present in my life," becoming instead a reality that is recognized in every passing act and thought. It is something that is discovered through discipline, a spiritual discipline, one of the best of which is that one so common and so often overlooked, the discipline of the life of the family, the spirituality of the center.

The presence of God—it is this that the spirituality of the family seeks to live; it is this that it seeks to teach. The time has come to recognize the family for the true spiritual discipline it is and so to develop it in a way that enhances its spiritual gifts. The spirituality of the family, of life at the center, is one of the most rigorous and most difficult, but it is also among the most rewarding and transforming of all of the great spiritual disciplines. For those seeking God who have the courage and strength to meet what it asks, this life can reveal the living truth of the presence of God as little else can. But it is a hard discipline; it asks much of those who seek to practice it. It asks for courage and perseverance, but what it reveals is the love and the holiness at the very core of all that is. It does this by asking that a person dedicate himself or herself to live the daily expression of two sacraments, the sacrament of the care of others and the sacrament of the routine. They are both hard sacraments to live, but within the first love is revealed and within the second the sacredness of ordinary activity. To live both together is to find in the truest manner possible the presence of God.

6. The Sacrament of the Care of Others

Dear God, whose name is Love, who in love and with love formed all that is, teach me to see the great worth of those small, everyday tasks involved in the care of others. Teach me to see them for what they are: re-enactments of the greatest truth there is, the truth of your unfailing care for me and for all that is.

It was a hot summer evening the day before my twenty-third birthday. The air was heavy and still. No breeze rustled the curtains of the open windows. My wife, Pamela, was nine months pregnant, our first child due any day. The night air itself seemed weighted with expectation and long waiting.

We sat in the kitchen, too restless to go to bed, too drained by heat and preoccupation with the pregnancy even to talk. I looked at my watch. It was nearly eleven-thirty.

"Would a walk help?" I asked, not expecting that it would.

Pamela considered.

"It might be cooler," she said.

It did seem cooler outside. The dark air even carried a hint of a breeze. We walked the country road that ran beside the house, listening to the restless unquiet of a rural night—the droning bass of bullfrogs, the screeches of the crickets—and we were drawn into a deeper stillness. Beyond the fields a neighboring farmhouse lay silent and dark. We were alone, and, suddenly refreshed, we walked side by side at a pace comfortable for Pamela; we passed field after field unaware of time or distance.

The road narrowed and turned into a wood. And suddenly we found ourselves standing in darkness so profound that we had to stop. Then all at once Pamela gripped my arm.

"What's going on?" she whispered.

But I was too stunned to answer. Suddenly the air came alive with lights as if we had been hurled into space and surrounded by stars, hundreds of stars, each many times brighter than any seen from earth, but stars that hovered and darted around us, blinking, shifting, darting—vanishing and returning—filling the whole of the sky. All at once I realized what they were.

"Fireflies."

I could hardly even speak the word. Was it really possible? Could they have appeared like this, all at once? And could there really be this many? Here, there, all around us, hundred upon hundred, each punctuated the heavy curtain of darkness so that the night itself seemed to glitter and sparkle.

"Amazing," my wife said beside me, so softly that I hardly heard. "It's simply incredible."

And there we stood, captured suddenly within a magical world, held by the beauty and wonder of it all. It was only years later that I recognized that evening as the true prelude to the day that was to follow.

When at last we returned, tired but peaceful, we went immediately to bed only to be awakened about five the next morning by a thunderstorm. The heat wave had broken and powerful winds were driving heavy rain into the windows we had left open. We jumped from bed to rush from room to room, stepping in the puddles already forming on the floor and slamming down the sashes so that the storm was left to pound against the glass.

When the windows were all closed and the floors dried, I returned to bed, falling asleep too soon to realize that Pamela had decided not to follow me. She awoke me two hours later with a birthday cake and orange juice.

"I never did this quite so early before," I said blowing out the candles sleepily.

"I wasn't sure you'd have a chance later on."

"What do you mean?"

All at once Pamela seemed impatient.

"We can cut the cake later," she said. "I have your birthday present in the attic. Why don't you carry it down."

The present turned out to be a bookcase she had commissioned a carpenter friend of ours to build for me. I carried it into the living room and together we began to assemble it. Once or twice she seemed to pause, as if made suddenly aware of something deep within her.

"Are you all right?" I asked.

The question brought her back sharply.

"Of course I am," she said, turning away from me.

With the bookcase assembled and books, which until then had been stored in boxes, carefully arranged along its shelves, I felt a sudden inspiration and began to suggest to Pamela all the various ways in which we might rearrange the furniture to make the room more attractive. In the middle of a sentence I stopped. Again a distant look passed over my wife's face, this time with a flicker of pain.

I watched her a moment.

"The baby's coming, isn't it," I said.

"I don't know. It's too early to tell."

"I better call the doctor."

"No wait. Wait until I can be sure."

But then she gripped the edge of a chair. The expression was unmistakable.

"I'm calling the doctor," I said.

"Well, if it would make you feel better . . ."

Over the phone I related what I had seen. I also reminded the doctor that we had an hour-and-a-half drive to the hospital. He suggested we come in.

I found Pamela sitting rubbing her stomach and panting in the manner she had been taught in classes preparing her for childbirth without drugs.

"The doctor said this might be it," I said.

She could only nod vigorously. Her eyes, locked onto mine, were wide with exhilaration and panic.

Weeks before I had put a mattress in the back of our small station wagon to be ready for this day. The drive into the city seemed endless. The classes in childbirth we had attended together had taught how to notice the beginning, the peak, and the decline of the contractions of labor. They had also suggested ways to meet the pain through a series of breathing and massaging exercises. While I drove as fast as I dared, Pamela lay in the back, panting with the quick, shallow breaths she had been taught, while frantically massaging her belly.

"Tell me when the next contraction begins," I called back to her.

"Now," she said quickly, beginning her panting once more.

I looked away from the road to check my watch.

"Tell me when it ends."

Contractions at the beginning of labor are short, with long intervals in between. As labor progresses the contractions become longer, the space between them shorter. The longer the contractions, the closer the baby is to being born. I watched in growing panic as the second hand of my watch jumped farther and farther around the dial, making a full circuit and still continuing.

"Is this still the same contraction?" I called back.

The sound of the rapid, shallow panting was her only answer. Only much later did we discover that the motion of the car was causing her enough discomfort that she was unable to distinguish it from the pain of the early contractions. At the time it seemed that Pamela was already in the advanced stages of labor.

"Let me hold your hand," she called up to me.

With one hand stretched behind me gripped tightly by Pamela with both of hers and the other on the steering wheel as we sped along the interstate, I began to rehearse in my mind what I would do if I had to deliver the baby myself.

But then we were in the city and parked before the hospital. We discovered after the nurse examined her that Pamela still had many hours to go before delivery.

Then the really hard work began. Sitting beside her I did the few small things I could—time contractions, help her stay with her breathing exercises, massage her back and legs—while she struggled through her long marathon of endurance. And watching her I thought often of the struggle of long-distance runners who continue mile after mile, step after step, long after fatigue has filled every muscle. The difference, though, was that where they might have stopped, she could not, and Pamela's race was longer and harder than any athlete would willingly endure.

Hours after arriving at the hospital we were still at it, and the only obvious change was that it was becoming more and more difficult. Pamela was so exhausted that she would begin to doze in the ten to fifteen seconds that she now had between contractions.

Then all at once something changed. Suddenly wide awake, she sat up and looked at me. The final stage of labor, the one just before the birth of the baby, would be marked, we had been told many times, by something always described as "an urge to push." This phrase had always bothered Pamela.

"Well, what exactly does it feel like?" she would ask. "I mean, how am I going to be sure that that is what it is? How will I recognize it?"

"Don't worry," each person had always answered. "When the time comes you will have no trouble recognizing it. You will have a sudden and overwhelming desire to push the baby out and that will mean that you are in the final stage of labor."

Pamela had remained skeptical. But here it was. In one instant she was fully alert. She looked at me, her eyes wide with surprise.

"They were right," she said. "I feel it. I want to push the baby out."

The nurse confirmed that it was time, and as she wheeled Pamela to the delivery room the doctor was already scrubbing up.

With both the doctor and nurse present I helped Pamela to sit up so that, working with the contraction, she could bear down harder. As each contraction ended she would lay back once more and rest, only to sit up again with the next. She had to do this only five or six times and the baby was born.

"A boy," the doctor said. "A healthy baby boy."

Pamela lay back and turned to me.

"Happy birthday," she said. "I'm afraid we never did get a chance to cut the cake, but I hope you like your present."

The nurse stared.

"She's joking, isn't she? It isn't really your birthday, is it?"

I nodded.

"My God," she muttered. "What can she possibly get for you next year?"

The doctor gave the baby to Pamela to hold briefly before the nurse took him. She then washed him, weighed him, and wrapped him in a blanket. When she returned, it was to me that she gave him.

And then suddenly I realized that it was for this, for this small baby, that all this had occurred. And at that moment it was a revelation. In the past nine months I had of course thought often of the baby, but it was simply that—"the baby"—something abstract and unreal. Now for the first time I met him, this tiny boy who, never visible, had been so much a part of our lives for so many months. I met him and saw him for the first time not as "the baby" but as a unique person. His eyes were open and he looked all around him, studying a world that was for him incomprehensible and unnamed. His hair was light. His hand had slipped outside the blanket. It was clenched into a tiny fist.

And then I felt again the awe and wonder of the sudden magic of the fireflies the evening before. Here, out of nowhere was a life. Where had it been in all those tens of thousands of years while other human beings were born, lived, and died and civilizations grew, flourished, and declined? Where had this life been then? And where was it going? What lay ahead for him in childhood, youth, and adulthood? And what was beyond? Where would he be in the eternal sequence of centuries that were still ahead? In a great wave of wonderment these questions washed over me, slowly to be replaced with something else, a feeling calmer, stiller. This I recognized at once, and in that instant knew that I loved this child, loved this tiny boy at this our first meeting, as I would from now onward. Where he had been or where he was going was uncertain, but that he was loved, was not. I knew then that Love endures.

But I also sensed, although in a much vaguer way, that this *feeling* of love was only part of what was involved. My task, my discipline, would be to learn to *express* this love, to learn not only to have it, but to give it. That was one of my first perceptions of the nature of that first half of the spirituality of the family, the sacrament of the care of others.

Love itself is a gift, a grace. It is something mysterious, given us by God. What we do with that love is up to us. Each of us must learn to express it and by expressing it cause it to grow, not just in us but in others—a candle kindling other candles.

This is the task of a lifetime. It is the heart of marriage, but it takes on a unique importance in parenthood. It is particularly important there, because whether a child will later be able to accept the gift of love when it is offered depends in large part on how much love the child knew in those years before he or she could recognize it for what it was. Learning the expression of love is also so supremely central to parenthood because it is there that it can become the most difficult to live day after day. Caring for a ten-month-old child who spits out every spoonful of food you give him; or for a two-year-old who, finding a scissors on the table decides that she is going to sew the way she has seen her mother do and going to the closet, cuts several sections out of two of her mother's best dresses; or for a teenager who for several months running has made a point of contradicting every word his parents say—caring for children in situations such as these draws on all that anyone can learn of love as something requiring courage and persistence.

Courage and persistence—these then are elements of the sacrament of the care of others. It is persistence that keeps a person working at a life expressing love when the rewards of such a life no longer seem clear, and it is courage that dares such commitment.

There are also other elements of this life. One is trust. Trust is the ability to receive and to give in turn. It is what allows a person both to help and to be helped, to be sometimes weak and sometimes strong. It is trust that allows a person to cultivate the vulnerability so essential to love.

Too often love is the word we use to justify control over others, just as too often it is also the word we use to mark surrender to such control. Love must involve a trust that permits the vulnerability that comes of being both for each other, both helper and helped. How easy it is to fall into a pattern in which one person is always giving direction. And yet when this continues, the relationship degenerates into a dull repetition of roles; all shared experience ends. In a real sense neither one is really a *person* to the other. For love to be complete, it must embrace the truth that every person is in some ways weak and in some ways strong, so that it is only by pretense or suppression that a person seems to appear always one or always the other.

"How do you know God loves you?" I and the others in a small group were asked. One person gave one answer, the next another. Finally a woman raised her hand, paused, and glanced at her husband who was sitting beside her watching her in turn.

"I think my husband and I both feel God's love for us most strongly in the love we have for each other. I can never doubt God's love for me when I see my husband's look of love and trust."

This is the sort of truly mutual love that only trust allows. It is a love that is balanced, a love that is powerful.

A fourth aspect of the expression of love is forgiveness. Forgiveness is renewal. It is love that seeks to find itself again after some incident or misunderstanding has seemed to obscure it. To forgive a person is different from excusing him. When a person asks to be excused for some small social blunder, it means that in effect a mutual pact is being formed where both sides agree to pretend as if nothing happened. Forgiveness is more profound. It does not so much ask that whatever went wrong be hidden from view, as that both persons involved actively renew the connection they had with one another. It is a return to the foundation of their love, a return that may involve stripping away some shoddy construction in the relationship, some false image that one was projecting of him- or herself or demanding of the other, returning to that foundation of care for each other that has God's love as its ultimate source. Forgiveness is what two people offer to each other not so much because of what has gone wrong, but for what they share.

Forgiveness is, then, a renewal, and for love to grow it must be renewed every day. This renewal is not one that seeks somehow to return to the past, however; rather, it seeks to revitalize the present. To carry a grudge is to live in the past, to live with the bitterness of disappointment or of the expectation of a future that never was. Both of these—the past that now is gone and the future that never was—are illusionary worlds. To live in them is to make encampments in deception. Forgiveness frees a person to live in the reality of the relationship's true present.

I know a child of nine who was on his way out the door to get his younger brother the Christmas present he had been saving for when he discovered that that very brother had just broken one of his own favorite toys. He flew into a rage.

"What were you doing with it?" he yelled. "You didn't even ask me if you could use it. And why weren't you more careful? Just for that you can never play with my toys again. And also, I've just decided that I'm not going to buy you a Christmas present this year." He stomped out of the room.

A moment later he returned to the kitchen and slipped on his coat. "I'm going, Mom," he said in a voice that in no way suggested the anger of a moment before.

"Going where?" his mother asked.

"To buy the present."

His mother couldn't hide her look of surprise.

"Well he *is* my brother, isn't he?"

Children live in the present. Forgiveness can be for them almost spontaneous. Adults find it more difficult. And yet adults can work toward something close to this ability of children; we can learn little by little to deal with people not according to what they may have done that we did not like, or according to the expectations we had for them that they did not meet, but according to who they are right now. That, after all, is the one true relationship.

In addition to courage, persistence, trust, and forgiveness there is a fifth element of the sacrament of the care of others: the ability to balance the tension between holding on and letting go. Both of these elements are always present in every close relationship, but in ways that shift from day to day.

Caring is holding. Children especially must be held and protected, but adults need this too. But caring is also letting go. It is releasing those we love to go in the direction they need to go and to develop in ways that may at times be perplexing to us their husbands, wives, parents, or friends, but ways essential to their growth. The difficulty comes in finding ways to do both of these, both holding and letting go, within the same relationship.

The general movement in parenthood is from holding—a holding that is almost constant in the early days—to letting go, although each stage of raising children involves a little of each. An eleven-month-old child just learning to walk is in a very real sense striking out on her own. As she balances herself to take one faltering step then another, the parent holding her hand must let go—let go both literally and figuratively. The struggle and the triumph must be hers alone, which can happen only if the parent for a moment moves aside. One step, then another, then another. She makes it across the room. In one small, essential way she has struck out on her own. A minute later she may try again, fall, and, crying, reach up and ask to be held, but this is the way of childhood. It involves for the child a long pattern of stepping out and returning, stepping out and returning, each time going further and further, developing more and more, always in ways that ask the parent to let go, then hold, let go, then hold—but each time to let go a bit more fully than before.

If in parenthood there is a general movement from holding to letting go, there is nothing so certain as this in marriage. One day one partner may need to be held. Something has happened that leaves him or her feeling hurt and alone. At that moment marriage becomes a protected place to which he or she may retreat and find comfort, encouragement, and safety. The next day, when confidence has returned, none of that is needed. Then marriage becomes a center from which to expand into far- and wide-ranging explorations. Everyone has times when he or she needs to be held and times when he or she needs to be let go. Marriage can provide a better place for this than anything else.

Courage, persistence, trust, forgiveness, and the ability to balance holding with letting go—these are the elements of the sacrament of the care of others. Put them together and what takes shape is the set of responses which are the *expression* of love. This sacrament of care is expressed not in grand gestures but in small acts which often go unnoticed. The true care that this life expresses is found in changing diapers, in standing in line with a five-year-old as he waits for the beginning of his first day of school, in reading a bedtime story to a child in first grade, then allowing her to read it back to you—halting, stumbling, but proud—and so demonstrate her newly found skill in reading. It is settling disputes, attending school plays. It is going through the entire drawer to find the match for a child's favorite sock. It is comforting a child when the older children won't let her play. It is helping with homework and admitting at times that you do not know the answer either. It is day after day spent in acts that let a child grow and change and holding and comforting him when he cannot.

It is a difficult life, difficult in the attentiveness and energy it asks. Care is constant. It is likely to be most needed at exactly those times you yourself feel least able to give it. It is difficult, too, because it asks you to see the extent of your own limitations.

But this life can be difficult for an entirely different reason. All of these never-ending, everyday tasks can seem far from what is most important in life and that probably more than anything else makes them hard to endure. It is not easy to see how each of these acts, so fleeting in itself, adds up to much more collectively. How hard it is to give yourself to something that seems to have so little significance! A scientist may work year after year in the most painstaking and meticulous accumulation of data. There is nothing at all exciting about the task itself, but his resolve never falters, his interest never fades, because he is convinced of the ultimate importance of what he does. In the same way an artist may work year after year without the smallest recognition. There is no encouragement, no support, but still she continues because she also is convinced that what she does is important. Some tasks are grueling, demanding, and repetitive but are done with enthusiasm. Others are varied and complex but viewed with scorn. It is seldom the nature of the work itself that determines our attitude toward it. That comes instead from our assessment of its ultimate value. And one of the greatest problems with the sacrament of caring is that so few—even those most deeply involved—see much in it that is special. Life at the center is an occupation without status. In parenthood especially, which moves so slowly but so inevitably to a more and more complete letting go, it is never finally clear what has been accomplished. After all those years, the scientist finally has his data; the contribution is made. The artist has her work; the achievement is there. But in the end, the children grown, what do parents have to show for what was done? They cannot point to a son or daughter and say, "I built this," the way a scientist can lay claim to a formula, an artist to a painting. It is one of those great mysteries of parenthood that although a mother and father make important contributions, very early a child begins to take a hand in her own formation so that the truly successful parent looking at a grown child cannot say so much "She is mine," as "She is herself."

Because the tasks are ordinary and of little alleged value in themselves and because they offer no clear achievement for which a person can take credit—these are the reasons that cause so many engaged in living the sacrament of caring to feel it is something of little worth. And yet no work in life has greater importance. Of course, caring for others, especially for children, is essential to the continued well-being of society. That is the sort of objective truth that everyone recognizes but that somehow never seems to make much difference in what a person actually feels about what he or she is doing. Caring for others is of course important to society, but what I want to talk about is the importance that such care has for the person actually giving it.

Living the sacrament of care for others draws a person close to the greatest of all truths. It does this better than anything else can, but it does this in ways that are seldom obvious. It is for this reason that it is a spiritual discipline. Those who first sought the desert and found themselves alone, with little food, little water, and nothing to stand between themselves and God, did not feel immediate inspiration. All they found at first was loneliness, hunger, thirst, and temptations. It was only later, after living their life with prayer and carefully listening to the words spoken within the heart, that they learned the truth hidden within the struggle they had chosen. The same is true here. Only after living the sacrament of care day after day and working as much as possible to find within it the aspect of prayer does this life begin to reveal itself as one joined to the most powerful truth there is.

It is then that the sacrament of caring reveals its special connection with God. To live this life is to participate in the mystery of the divine and to become a partner in that ongoing act of creation, the forming of the love from which all else is formed. Because this is done so closely with God it never becomes the sort of thing a person can ever truly claim as his or her own, as a scientist might claim of his work or an artist of hers. Perhaps even the scientist and artist are wrong to make such claims, but what they do seems enough their own that no one would argue with them. But a parent, a spouse, a friend—the creation that each of these forms within the heart of those they love is invisible to all and never recognized by anyone, except perhaps the one to whom the love is given.

It is hard, then, to see this love as something unique. And yet it is. The love each person forms and gives to another is unlike anything ever found before or since. It is one with the person who forms it. Although drawn from something deeper, it has been elaborated and expanded in ways that no one else could do. It is one of a kind, at once something unduplicated anywhere in the universe and also an expression of the deepest and most persistent truth of that universe. It is both its own and joined with everything else. It alone will survive. Paint fades and chips away; buildings crumble and decay; governments form, fall, and are forgotten; the pages of books yellow and turn to dust; and the great cosmic activities that scientific principles are meant to express continue long after the formulas themselves and the brains that formed them are forgotten and consigned to oblivion. All that passes. Only love and what love forms endure. What Grandfather or Sarah gave with their courage and their unhesitating care to all of those who knew them will ripple outward into wider and wider circles, from generation to generation, never to vanish, continuing long after all those who might remember its source are gone.

How the formation of love continues and grows in ways that nothing can hinder can be seen in the life of a woman whose story the world is now coming to know well. The woman was born in Yugoslavia in 1910 and christened Agnes Gouxha Bojaxhin, one of three children, the daughter of a grocer. By twelve she had resolved that her life would be spent helping the poor and the sick and at eighteen she sought entry into the congregation of Loreto nuns whose center of missionary activity was in Bengal. She was sent to Darjeeling, India, and worked as a teacher in the Loreto convent school, teaching the children of relatively well-off European and Indian families. When she took her final vows in 1931 she adopted the name by which the world would come to know her, Teresa.

She was soon sent to the high school for girls run by the Loreto Sisters in Calcutta. Calcutta is a city notorious for its slums and its poverty, but the school itself was removed from that. She worked hard to do the best she could with whatever work she was given to do, but she felt a nagging sense of something unresolved.

It was in 1946 that she had what she would later describe as "the call within a call." The country was torn at this time by fierce fighting between Hindus and Moslems—fighting that in Calcutta, made up of almost equal numbers of each, was particularly bloody. The misery that had always plagued that crowded city mounted horribly as the bodies of the mutilated and the murdered were left to lie among those dying of starvation and disease. It was in the middle of this brutal and dangerous time, that Teresa heard, clear and unmistakable, a call to give up what she was doing to go into the slums and serve the poorest of the poor.

She exchanged the habit of her order which she had worn for so many years for a simple *sari,* the dress of Indian women. Hers was of cheap white cloth with a blue border. This garment, with its small cross pinned to the left shoulder, would become her trademark and the trademark of the thousands of women who were eventually to follow as her Missionaries of Charity.

Alone, she entered a city of two hundred and fifty thousand lepers and three thousand abandoned children—these only a small part of a population grown numb with sickness and hunger. Her first action was to start a school, a school that met in a small open space between crowded huts where children squatted on the dirt and where Teresa used a stick to write in the mud the words they were to learn. The school started with five children, but every evening Teresa visited home after home, looking for those she might help. Slowly the school grew.

But the work for which she is most famous began in 1952 when she found a woman dying in the street and carried her herself to the hospital, then refused to leave until the hospital, which preferred to save their beds for others for whom there would be some hope of recovery or hope of payment, at last accepted her. As she tells it:

The first woman I saw I myself picked up from the street. She had been half eaten by the rats and ants. I took her to the hospital but they could not do anything for her. They only took her in because I refused to move until they accepted her. From there I went to the municipality and I asked them to give me a place where I could bring these people because on the same day I had found other people dying in the streets. The health officer of the municipality took me to the temple, the Kali Temple, and showed me the *dormashalah* where the people used to rest after they had done their worship of Kali goddess. It was an empty building; he asked me if I would accept it. I was very happy to have that place for many reasons, but especially knowing that it was a center of worship and devotion of the Hindus. Within twenty-four hours we had our patients there and we started the work of the home for the sick and dying who are destitutes. Since then we have picked up over twenty-three thousand people from the streets of Calcutta of which about fifty percent have died.[2]

The building has become a place of refuge for those who have nowhere at all to go—the beggar who collapses in the street, the leper disowned by his family, those turned away by the hospitals because of their hopeless conditions and poverty. All receive food, medical care, and for the many for whom nothing else is possible, a quiet place to die and the parting rituals of their own faith. It is a simple thing really. It is also the most profound gesture a human being can perform. As Teresa says:

First of all we want to make them feel that they are wanted, we want them to know that there are people who really love them, who really want them, at least for the few hours that they have to live, to know human and divine love. That they too may know that they are the children of God, and that they are not forgotten and that they are loved and cared about and there are young lives ready to give themselves in their service.[3]

Years after this and many other of her projects were well established and attracting women and men from all over the world who, inspired by her example, wanted to help her with her work, the little woman now known universally as Mother Teresa came to the United States. I heard her speak and was mesmerized. A tiny woman whose face seemed creased with every sorrow she had seen, whose nose was like a tulip bulb, and whose dark eyes sat within dark hollows—she could have been an old lady from a fairy tale. But her face was so alive. She smiled, and the wrinkles were immediately revealed to be etched not by sorrow but by joy. The dark hollows of her eyes seemed filled with the deepest sympathy and love.

Among the groups to which she spoke was one of religious sisters from many North American orders. After her talk she asked if there were any questions.

"Yes, I have one," a woman sitting near the front said. "As you know, most of the orders represented here have been losing members. It seems that more and more women are leaving all the time. And yet your order is attracting thousand upon thousand. What do you do?"

Without hesitating Mother Teresa answered, "I give them Jesus."

"Yes I know, but take habits, for example. Do your women object to wearing habits? And the rules of the order, how do you do it?"

"I give them Jesus."

"Yes, I know Mother, but can you be more specific?"

"I give them Jesus."

"Mother, we are all of us aware of your fine work. I want to know about something else."

"I give them Jesus. There is nothing else."

This is the essence of the sacrament of caring, giving Jesus to others. It is something that Mother Teresa has made her way of life, just as have all those who have adopted the spirituality of life at the center. But to truly give Jesus to others we must first find Jesus within ourselves. The gift of love by which we bind ourselves to the eternal must be discovered as our own before it can be given away. To discover Jesus within us is to discover the love God has for each of us. It is a love that can be difficult to accept simply because it is so vast as to be overwhelming. It is not always easy to see the extent of God's love, because to do that involves coming to know the entirety of the person to whom the love is given, the person each of us is. We are reluctant to see how much God loves us not out of humility, but out of pride. Each of us secretly wants to be perfect. Many of us carefully avoid looking at those aspects of ourselves that seem to us to be less than perfect. But to really know God's love, these aspects must be acknowledged simply because they too are part of what God loves. We resist being loved so fully. We say to God, "Wait, don't love me yet. Wait until I am worthy of your love. Don't love me in my weakness, in my pettiness, in my rashness. Wait a while and I will rid myself of these. *Then* you can love me. Right now I am too much like everyone else. If you love me as I am now, you might be tempted to love those others in the same way. Wait until I am better than those others. Then love me."

This is not God's way. To see the extent of God's love requires that you really know who it is that God loves—yourself. It means looking into your own greatness and into your own smallness and seeing that it is for both that God cares for you. To discover this love is humbling and liberating. It shows you exactly who you are, then fills you with an extraordinary energy as you find the ability, perhaps for the first time, to love that person. And once discovered, this love opens you to love others in the same way. It is the first step to finding Jesus. It is also the first step to giving Jesus to someone else.

7. The Sacrament of the Routine: The Sacred in the Ordinary

Dear God, it is in the small acts that I show you who I am. The grand gestures I do for others. I offer the small ones for you since you alone will notice. I give them to you, each act another word in the most complete prayer I can offer to you, the prayer that is my life.

The spirituality of the family is based on the care of others, and that care consists primarily of countless small tasks. Each is apparently insignificant in itself, but every one must be done again and again. Care is accomplished in the routine and the ordinary. It is washing a pile of dishes, all of which were washed several hours earlier; it is cleaning rooms cleaned just the day before but now unrecognizable under a cover of wooden blocks and other toys. It is getting up morning after morning to drive to a job you do not like but must continue in order to pay the bills. It is washing, cooking, driving—many acts small in themselves (and all the more difficult to take seriously for that very reason) piled one on top of the other, day after day, week after week without change.

It is the bland and repetitious part of life at the center that seems its greatest defect; the reality of a life of care often seems as far from spirituality as possible. It is true that it is the greatest burden of this life, but it is *not* true that it is far from spirituality. Spirituality is what draws a person closer to God, which means that it is also what draws a person closer to his or her own humanness, since it is in that that God's will is expressed in each of our lives. Spirituality is anything that reveals how close God is to us—as close as our hands, as close as our heart. It shows, as is written in Deuteronomy, that God's will is a reality that is not too hard for you, neither is it far off. It is not in heaven, that you should say, "Who will go up for us to heaven, and bring it to us, that we may hear it and do it?" Neither is it beyond the sea, that you should say, "Who will go over the sea for us, and bring it to us, that we may hear it and do it? But the word is very near you; it is in your mouth and in your heart, so that you can do it."[1]

Spirituality reveals how close God's truth is to us. It does this not simply by stating the truth, but by slowly drawing it into our lives. After all, something is not accepted as true simply with a nod of the head or even by a public profession. It is accepted as true only when its truth enters a person's very being. This may happen slowly, and it may not come easily. It is in the rigors of spirituality that truth is born, because it is there that it becomes not just another piece of the mind's furniture but something with blood and bone. In the spirituality of the family those rigors are found in the living out of the sacrament of the routine, that is, the slow discovery that the routine *is* a sacrament, the discovery of what is one of the most profound truths it is possible to know, the truth of the sacredness of the ordinary.

How the routine can become a spiritual discipline can be glimpsed in the life of a man known as Brother Charles of Jesus. He was born Charles Eugene Viscount de Foucauld in 1858. Both his parents died before his seventh birthday and he was raised by relatives.

A questioning, searching boy, he suddenly discovered at age sixteen that, in his words, his "faith was quite dead." He entered the Special Military School at Saint-Cyr. His academic work was exceptional. He was made a Lieutenant and sent to Algeria, but in less than a year he was dismissed for the wild unrestraint of his habits and his contemptuous disregard for discipline. When he discovered that his regiment was about to be sent to fight an insurrection, he pleaded to be reinstated to his former position. This he kept only as long as the fighting continued; then he resigned his commission.

During all this time Charles's absence of faith was a persistent and controlling reality in his life. He writes:

For twelve years I lived without any faith whatever: nothing seemed to me to be sufficiently proven: the same level of faith which inspired so many different religions really went to show that all of them were futile. . . . I was twelve years believing and denying nothing, despairing of the truth, and not even believing in God, as I was convinced by none of the proofs for his existence.[2]

But during his campaigns in North Africa he was confronted by something other than proofs to be accepted or denied. He met certain Jews and Muslims whose profound religious faith deeply moved him, bringing his own unbelief into question. Seeing the strength and power of the convictions of these people and the strength and power that filled their lives as a result, he began to see his scepticism—and the life he lived as its expression—not as the suave, intelligent response to unanswerable questions he had always assumed it to be, but something rather pale and even pathetic. "Islam shook me deeply . . . ," he writes, "seeing such faith, seeing people living in the continual presence of God, I came to glimpse something bigger and more real than worldly occupations."[3]

Returning to Paris, he began a period of study and searching. He read the great philosophers of ancient Greece and Rome, looking for a clue as to how he was to give his own life the sort of meaning he had seen in these others. Instead he found in them "nothing but emptiness and disgust." It was finally his cousin Marie—Madame de Bondy—who gave him direction. She gave him Christian books which, as he writes, were the first to make him "feel that there I might perhaps find if not truth (I did not believe men could know the truth), at least instruction in the path of virtue."[4] But more important than the books she gave was the life she herself was living. Here was an intelligent, educated woman who not only believed the teachings of her religion but found in them a source for the same kind of inspiration and devotion he had first admired in the Jews and Muslims of North Africa. This alone led to what were for him strange thoughts:

The first was an inspired thought: since this person is so intelligent, the religion she believes in with such devotion cannot be the foolishness I thought. The second was another inspired thought: since religion is not foolishness, perhaps it is the home of truth which has no other on earth among religions or the philosophical systems?[5]

At the age of twenty-eight he was converted and began instruction with a Father Havelin, a deeply prayerful man who became his lifelong spiritual director. The year was 1886.

In 1890 he joined the Cistercians, the order that fifty years later would attract Thomas Merton. He asked to be sent to the poorest of all the Cistercian monasteries and so was sent to one in Akbes, Syria, where he remained for seven years. But it is there that he began to be haunted by "that little life of Nazareth"—the hidden life of Jesus, the one Jesus lived in obscurity before his public ministry began, when he was an ordinary worker going about his daily routine. There his ministry was something unspoken yet proclaimed in the integrity of expression of the work he performed and the openness and love with which he dealt with those whose daily tasks he shared. More and more Brother Charles wanted to share this life of simplicity, obscurity, and routine. Finally in 1897 he received permission from the Abbot General of the order to travel to Nazareth. He writes:

I'm longing to start on that life I've been looking for for seven years, the life . . . I glimpsed, felt, as I walked through the streets of Nazareth where our Lord had trod, a poor workman lost in self-effacement and obscurity.[6]

He found work doing any of the menial tasks that had to be done at a convent of nuns in Nazareth. He was gardner, servant, and handyman. For him each task became an expression of profound truth. In 1897 he writes:

I am settled in Nazareth. . . . Here, as completely as I could possibly hope for, I have found, by God's grace, what I was looking for: poverty, solitude, self-effacement, humble work, complete obscurity, the most perfect possible imitation of the life of our Lord Jesus as he must have lived it in Nazareth. . . . I have embraced the humble and obscure existence of God, the worker of Nazareth.[7]

This was the life he had sought. This was his inspiration. Eventually he became a priest and moved to an isolated part of the Sahara, the only priest in two hundred and fifty miles, serving the few people who lived in that desolate land, nomads and a few French soldiers. There he wrote a book of twenty-one talks to explain God's word, calling it the *Gospel Presented to the Poor of the Sahara.* There he wrote his *Rule of the Little Brothers,* a plan for an order that would not have a single member in his lifetime but that later would flourish. There, too, he was murdered in 1916 by a band of terrorists who feared his influence. But in all of this his inspiration was in that "hidden life" he found in Nazareth.

It was hidden in one sense, in that it sought nothing but the simplest tasks; but in another sense it was anything but hidden, for a life that performs the ordinary, repetitious acts of the day and finds them not meaningless but expressions of a sacred truth, is a life so awesome that it cannot help being noticed. During every day that he lived, Charles de Foucauld was, as he himself says, "shouting the Gospel from the rooftop of his life." It was heard, heard in a way that it would not have been had he spoken only with his mouth and not with his hands, his arms, his back. Brother Charles spoke to many with his life, but what may be the hardest to understand is the great joy this life brought to him. He had broken through into that transforming and eternal moment when he knew the sacredness of everything he did, where everything was fresh and new and beautiful because it was done for God. He writes:

The soul who lives by faith is full of fresh thoughts, fresh tastes, fresh judgments, fresh horizons open up before him (. . .). Wrapped round by these new truths of which the world has no inkling, he necessarily starts on a new life which the world thinks madness. The world lies in darkest night, the man of faith basks in a brilliant splendour. The bright path he treads is unseen by man, he seems to them to be setting off into emptiness like the fool he is.[8]

He lived the discipline and knew the joys of the sacrament of the routine. And the fact that the discovery could be made through a life such as his shows that it is not the exclusive property of the spirituality of the family. And yet it is there, in the family, that it finds its fullest expression.

Charles de Foucauld found what the spirituality of the family is best able to teach, the sacredness of the routine and the ordinary. It is a great truth, perhaps one of the greatest a person can discover in realizing the full magnitude of his or her own worth, but it is a truth that does have to be *discovered*. It is not obvious. And simply stated in this way it can seem no more than pious drivel, or worse —something to keep people content with things with which no one can be content. It is not this, but the living reality of its truth words alone cannot convey.

The truth of the sacredness of the ordinary must be experienced to have any meaning. Without that experience words describing it can only seem puzzling and suspect. But for most of those caring for a family this routine is experienced not as something sacred, only as something oppressive. It is the very ordinariness of the tasks done day after day that most wear one down, burdening one with fatigue, drudgery, and boredom. If this is the only way the routine is experienced, it seems nothing but an attempt to sugar-coat something basically bad-tasting to say that there is a sacredness to ordinary and repetitious tasks.

It is not sugar-coating. But the full truth of these words can only be uncovered slowly, as the reality to which they point begins to be experienced. The words and life of Charles de Foucauld call us to consider that such an experience is possible, although it must be cultivated. The spirituality of the family can become the means to do this. There *is* a sacrament of the routine. Those caring for others always come to know the hardship. The call here is for them to also learn to know the beauty.

There are three stages to the development of the experience of the sacrament of the routine. The first stage is that of hearing, the second that of discipline, the third that of awareness. In the first stage the sacrament of the routine is first recognized as possibility. In the second stage one lives with the ordinary day after day, most often feeling it as ordinary, but working to discover the sacredness it expresses. The third stage offers the perceptive breakthrough when the truth of what had first been heard and then cultivated comes to be a frequently felt reality.

The first stage, then, is hearing. What is heard at this point will not make sense. Many will immediately reject it as nonsense for that very reason. Some, however, will decide that maybe, just maybe, it points to something very real that they have simply not experienced.

In Zen Buddhism this hearing begins with a *koan*. A *koan* is a sort of puzzle. It is a request or a question that requires a response, but not the sort of response that could ever be anticipated by logical thought. One well-known koan is, "Show me the face you had before your parents were born." Another is, "What is the sound of one hand clapping?" Koans do not ask for answers; they ask for insight, for awareness. But for that it is necessary to live with the koan day after day until suddenly the solution is obvious, a solution that explains not only the question but something about the person being questioned. Understanding comes when an idea is comprehended; to understand something, a person asks or is asked questions. Insight comes when a person discovers a new way of being; to find insight a person is asked a koan. Koans do not themselves give the insight, but they name the manner of inquiry and so open the way for people to find the insight for themselves.

Koan is a Japanese word, and koans have been used most explicitly in Buddhism; but Christianity also has its koans. Jesus' parables work as koans. They too defy easy interpretation. They were meant to be absorbed into a person's consciousness, initiating a recognition of a new way of seeing that eventually leads to transforming insight.

Several years ago a Zen master was visiting the United States from Japan. He was invited to tour a Trappist monastery in New England and was delighted by what he found there. Astonished by the life of prayer and quiet withdrawal he said through his interpreter:

"I had no idea that any Christians took silent prayer so seriously. There is much here in common with Zen."

So captivated was he that he offered to lead the entire monastery in a week long Zen retreat. Now, a Zen retreat is a vigorous affair. It requires up to ten hours of silent meditation a day—half-hour segments of unbroken contemplation each followed by five minutes of slow walking. There are some work periods and some time for the chanting of prayers, but it is the contemplation that fills the day. And other than the spoken prayers, no talking is allowed, with the exception of a daily interview with the master in which each monk is checked on his progress with his individual koan.

It was this sort of retreat the Zen master offered them, except that it would be, he said, adapted to particularly Christian insight. The monastery accepted his offer and he began his retreat, joining the monks for Mass, standing with them to say the offices, encouraging them to use chairs for silent meditation rather than the sitting position Japanese use and Westerners often find painful. In many ways he adapted his retreat to those he was leading. He also searched the New Testament for Christian koans.

At the first interview the monks were given their koans. When the first monk entered the room he found the Zen master sitting with two copies of the New Testament in front of him, one in English, one in Japanese. Because his English was imperfect he went from one to the other.

The monk sat down in front of him and the Zen master smiled.

"You know," he said in his faltering English, "I like Christianity. But—" he glanced down at the books in front of him, then looked up again, "I would not like it without the resurrection."

Suddenly he leaned forward so that his face was only inches from the other.

"Show me *your* resurrection," he said. He paused then, and smiled. "That is your koan. Show me your resurrection."

The koan is a good one. It cuts to the core of Christian belief. If, as Paul says, each Christian has already died and risen with Christ, then that resurrection must be part of our lives, visible for all to see. If we have it, we should be able to show it. If we cannot show it, perhaps we never really found it. Once found, it transforms each action into sacred ritual—each act, each deed becomes an expression of worship of the divine energy that formed each of us and formed the world. To live the resurrection that we as Christians have already undergone is to turn all of life into prayer and so turn all that is done, all that is said, into a long litany of praise for God.

But to see that this is so is still only the first stage of learning the sacrament of the routine. It is only to have been given the koan, not to have solved it. The insight that brings the full awareness very seldom follows immediately upon first hearing. Most often the hearing is followed by a long secondary stage, that of discipline. Here the truth that there is something sacred in every act is recognized, but not felt. It is when a person has given assent to this truth but still day after day goes by and all that he or she does seems just as mundane as ever. The alarm goes off in the pale light of morning and another day of work lies ahead. The dishes are piled by the sink, to be washed once again. The child cries and the telephone rings, the floor must be washed—where, one asks, is the sacred in any of this?

This is where the discipline of the sacrament of the routine is revealed. To recognize the *fact* that there is something sacred in the ordinary is only to plant a seed. The seed must be allowed to grow. It must be tended so that little by little it can develop into the full, living reality. And like a seed which, once planted, lies buried for weeks, months, or even years with nothing visible, this truth, once planted in the consciousness, will appear invisible to the heart, a truth not yet really true since it is without life. But if tended long enough, it will begin to show itself. Again, like a plant, it will be at first small and fragile but will in time grow stronger.

"Look at the mustard seed," Jesus said. "The smallest of seeds, it grows to a great plant." To look at the seed, that it produces such a plant seems impossible, and yet from such comes a full-grown plant, large and strong. For some people such awareness seems to grow of itself, a wildflower that takes root in their hearts. Others have to tend more carefully.

I know of one man who, as soon as he awakes in the morning, says to himself, "This is the day the Lord has made, I will rejoice and be glad." He continues to say this whenever there is a lull in the day or he feels a need to renew his strength. At first it was often little more than rote repetition, but gradually every time he said it to himself he began to see how true it was. "Today *is* the day the Lord has made," he would think. "I *will* rejoice and be glad." It became a certainty that lingered in his consciousness long after the prayer had been said.

Living with this prayer is one form the discipline can take. Similar to it is the discipline of the "Jesus Prayer," the prayer of the heart. The story of how this prayer altered one man's life is told in *The Way of a Pilgrim.* The man whose story it is does not reveal his name; he is simply the pilgrim. He does, however, reveal some of his history.

Born in a small village in Russia in the nineteenth century, the pilgrim was orphaned when he was two. He was raised by his grandparents. The family was poor but the grandfather was fortunate enough to have learned to read. When an injury so crippled the boy that he lost the use of one of his hands and it became clear that he would never be able to perform manual labor, the grandfather taught him to read too, hoping to give him a chance at other employment. The only book they read together was the Bible.

The pilgrim was not quite twenty when his grandparents died. He soon married, but not long afterward their house was burned down by a man who had broken in while they slept to steal what little money they had. The pilgrim and his wife escaped by climbing out the window. They had the clothes on their backs and the Bible he had inherited from his grandfather, which he had kept near him at night. Everything else was destroyed. They tried to start again, borrowing money to build a small house, but not long afterward the pilgrim's wife suddenly came down with a high fever. Nine days later she was dead. After a lifetime of tragedy this sorrow was simply too great for the man to bear:

I was overwhelmed with sorrow for my wife, and when I would come into the house and notice her scarf or some other piece of her clothing, I would weep until I fell unconscious. When I could no longer bear the grief of living at home, I sold the house for twenty rubles and gave whatever clothes there were, both my wife's and mine, to the poor. Then, because of my handicap I was given a free passport, so I took my beloved Bible and set out where my eyes would lead.[9]

He wandered from place to place until one Sunday he sat in church where the reading was taken from Paul's first letter to the Thessalonians. From the passage two words seemed to leap out at him and take hold of his mind. "Pray constantly," Paul had written, and these words, heard so often before, suddenly seemed a command he had no choice but to obey. But how, he thought, was this possible? How was he to pray continuously, without stop? It seemed beyond human capacity, and yet he had no doubt that he must somehow find a way to do so.

From then on, wherever he wandered he sought out those who might know and asked them whether they could teach him to pray without ceasing. Finally he heard of a monastery with a Superior known for his wisdom and devotion. He journeyed there and was taken inside and offered refreshments. But he was unable to contain himself:

"Reverend Father," I said, "I do not need refreshments, but I would like you to give me spiritual advice. . . . I heard that it is necessary to pray without ceasing, but I do not know how to pray without interruption and I cannot even understand what is meant by ceaseless prayer. Please explain this to me, dear Father."[10]

The elder told the man about a book called the *Philokalia,* in which the writings of twenty-five theologians on ceaseless prayer had been compiled. Its purpose was to give instruction on how to follow Paul's suggestion to pray continuously. The elder went on:

"Now if you will listen, I will read how you can learn ceaseless interior prayer." The elder opened the *Philokalia* to the account of St. Simeon the New Theologian and began reading. " 'Sit alone and in silence; bow your head and close your eyes; relax your breathing and with your imagination look into your heart; direct your thoughts from your head into your heart. And while inhaling say, "Lord Jesus Christ, have mercy on me," either softly with your lips or in your mind. Endeavor to fight distractions but be patient and peaceful and repeat this process frequently.' "[11]

Delighted to have an answer to his question at last, the pilgrim began that very evening. He found that as simple as the prayer was, it was often far from easy to keep going. The elder encouraged him. He spent time, as the book directed, in silent withdrawal, concentrating without distractions on the prayer alone, but he also found that he could continue the silent repetition of the prayer when he was doing other things too. Eventually he began to experience through the prayer what he described as "a kind of blessed warmth in the heart which spread throughout my whole breast."[12] It seemed as if he were now saying the prayer with his heart as well as his mind. It had become a constant activity, one like breathing that seemed to continue on its own without effort. The prayer had become one with him, fused with everything he did:

I got so accustomed to the prayer of the heart that I practiced it without ceasing and finally I felt that the Prayer of itself, without any effort on my part, began to function both in my mind and heart; it was active both day and night without the slightest interruption, regardless of what I was doing. My soul praised God and my heart overflowed with joy.[13]

Many things were beginning to change in the man:

Periodically, I began to experience various feelings and perceptions in my heart and mind. Sometimes I felt a sweet burning in my heart and such ease, freedom, and consolation that I seemed to be transformed and caught up in ecstasy. Sometimes I experienced a burning love toward Jesus Christ and all of God's creation. Sometimes I shed joyful tears in thanksgiving to God for His mercy to me, a great sinner. Sometimes difficult concepts became crystal clear and new ideas came to me which of myself I could not have imagined. Sometimes the warmth of the heart overflowed throughout my being and with tenderness I experienced God's presence within me. Sometimes I felt great joy in calling on the name of Jesus Christ and I realized the meaning of the words, "The Kingdom of God is within you" (Luke 17:21).

These and similar consolations led me to conclude that the fruits of the prayer of the heart can be experienced in three ways in the spirit, in the emotions, and in revelations. In the spirit one can experience the sweetness of the Love of God, inner peace, purity of thought, awareness of God's presence, and ecstasy. In the emotions a pleasant warmth of the heart, a feeling of delight throughout one's being, joyful bubbling in the heart, lightness and courage, joy of life and indifference to sickness and sorrow. And in revelation one receives the enlightment of the mind, understanding of Holy Scripture, knowledge of speech of all creatures, renunciation of vanities, awareness of the sweetness of interior life, and confidence in the nearness of God and His love for us.[14]

There was one other result of the prayer of the heart. Not only did it transform the man himself, altering him and his perception of his relation with God, but he saw all of creation with new eyes, so that

everything around me became transformed and I saw it in a new and delightful way. The trees, the grass, the earth, the air, the light, and everything seemed to be saying to me that it exists to witness to God's love for man and that it prays and sings of God's glory.[15]

It is through such discipline as this that truth is transformed from something merely heard but not understood into something that touches the core of a person's being. For some, the discipline of living a life of caring for others is itself enough to draw them from hearing to awareness. Its constant focus on the expression of love becomes so steadily a mirror of that divine love that in the end the two become joined in the heart of the one giving that love to others. Many others—by far the majority of us, I suspect—need some aid to remind us daily and hourly that the care we are giving to others *has* this fuller contact, that it *does* reflect this greater love. Short, simple prayers such as, "Today is the day the Lord has made, I will rejoice and be glad," "Lord Jesus Christ, have mercy on me," or any others, if repeated from the heart in times of quiet reflection and continued as a backdrop to all activity, can do this; they can draw a person's attention to God in a way that the very nature of awareness is transformed. By bringing prayer to everything done, everything done becomes prayer. This is awareness, the final stage.

A person begins, then, with a sense that everything he or she does is ordinary and routine. It does not matter that there may be some who see something special in it, to this individual it is mundane and bland. He or she longs for something unusual, something sacred to enter life. It seems so far away. Hearing that the ordinary is sacred makes it seem no closer. But through long discipline there come moments when the sacred is felt within the routine. At first these are only glimpses. But more and more frequently the sacredness of ordinary work is felt until at last the sacred and the routine become one—the sacred now routine, the routine sacred. To live this is to have found the answer to the koan, "Show me your resurrection." It is to know what Paul meant when he said that as Christians we have already been raised with Christ even as we also wait for the full transformation. It is to discover, as a man known as Brother Lawrence wrote over three hundred years ago, that "it is not necessary to be always in church to be with God, we can make a private chapel of our heart where we can retire from time to time to commune with him peacefully, humbly, lovingly."[16]

And in this man, Brother Lawrence, it is possible to see how fully this realization can grow from a life of routine care for others. Brother Lawrence was born Nicholas Herman in Hérimesnil in the Lorraine region of France. The most commonly cited date for his birth is 1611. About his early years almost nothing is known except that his parents were particularly religious and that at eighteen he joined the army. This was during the Thirty Years' War. Frequent skirmishes were taking a heavy toll on all sides. Soldiers were in constant demand.

At one point he was captured and about to be hung as a spy until he managed to convince those who held him that he was simply an unlucky soldier of the other side. He was released and returned to his unit but was later wounded in a Swedish raid. The wound was serious enough to end his military career, but he returned home haunted by memories of the carnage and brutality he had seen.

He worked for a time as a footman to one of the nobility but then decided to withdraw from the world as a hermit. This, however, lasted for only a short period.

After giving up the life of a hermit, he returned to Paris and applied for admission as a lay brother at a monastery of Discalced Carmelites. He was professed two years later, in 1642, and given the name by which he would be known from then on, Brother Lawrence of the Resurrection.

He worked in the monastery kitchen. For thirty years he prepared all the meals for the other monks, until a persistent gout which had plagued him painfully for years worsened to the point where he was barely able to stand. Then he was given the job of repairing shoes. A large man, he described himself as "a clumsy lummox." He had a directness that was sometimes misinterpreted as gruffness, but he was also gentle, kind, open—the warmest of human beings. He was to all appearances a simple man performing tasks no different than those done by most of the men and women who have lived and died upon the earth. But what set him apart was that he saw the extraordinary within the ordinary, the sacred in the routine. His insights into work and prayer were recorded by an Abbé Joseph de Beaufort, who kept notes of several conversations he and Brother Lawrence had together and joined these with a small collection of Brother Lawrence's letters to form a little book called *The Practice of the Presence of God*. It is in these conversations, set down in the shorthand manner that gives Brother Lawrence's thoughts in terse phrases, that is possible to glimpse the full realization of the sacrament of the routine, the awareness of God ever present.

He notes that for Brother Lawrence,

the time of prayer was no different from any other time, that he retired to pray when Father Prior told him to do so, but that he neither desired nor asked for this since his most absorbing work did not divert him from God. [17]

And that

he was more united to God in his ordinary activities than when he devoted himself to religious activities which left him with a profound spiritual dryness.[18]

Brother Lawrence believed that

our sanctification depended not upon changing our works but in doing for God what we ordinarily do for ourselves. . . .

[He found] that the best way of reaching God was by doing ordinary tasks, which he was obliged to perform under obedience, entirely for the love of God and not for the human attitude toward them.

[For him] it was a great delusion to think that time set aside for prayer should be different from other times, . . . [since] we were equally obliged to be united to God by work in the time assigned to work as by prayer during prayer time.[19]

Brother Lawrence died in 1691 and yet I feel almost as if I have known him. When I read how he welcomed all, the great and the humble without distinction, and opened himself to them, talked with them and helped them in any way he could, I think of Grandfather welcoming and caring for all who came to him. When I hear how Brother Lawrence claimed that, for him, to cook was to pray, I think of Sarah baking her bread carefully and lovingly. Although done thousand upon thousand times already, she kneads the dough, lets it rise, bakes, and watches for it to turn just the right shade of golden brown with such careful attention that those with her have no doubt they are witnessing an act of worship.

The common element in all three of these lives is the realization of a truth so true as to be almost universally overlooked, that life has one purpose above all others—to give love to God and to those near you and to allow yourself to be loved in turn. Any work that expresses this love is great work, any that does not is nothing. There is nothing we can do, not anything at all, that rivals this in importance. We are called first to find the depth of love, then its breadth. To have loved deeply, profoundly, fully, even one other human being, and to have welcomed his or her love in return, expresses the essence of all that life contains.

It is with love that the sacrament of the routine transforms the ordinary into the sacred. It is this that Brother Lawrence discovered. He knew "that we should not weary of doing little things for the love of God who looks not at the grandeur of these actions but rather at the love with which they are performed."[20] He knew that there is nothing great about great deeds if they are done without love. The movements of nations, the cheers of the crowds, the enactment of laws, the creation of governments—even laws and governments intending the general good—all of these are nothing beside a life lived for love. Every loving act is a grand gesture, one that sets the universe ajar and finds an answer from the source that is the origin of eternity.

Without love even those deeds that earn prestige, wealth, and power become hollow and empty. With love, the smallest, most ordinary of actions becomes sacred. But love is not something that we can will in ourselves, not something we can force ourselves to have. Some love we seem to be born into, as with the love of a child for her parents. Other love seems to take us by surprise, as with the romantic love which comes, as the expression has it, when we "fall in love." But neither of these loves, powerful as they can be, are alone enough to transform the totality of life in that way that makes every act into sacred ritual. For such as this, love must be mined in a way that opens it into an expression of that eternal love we have so long called by the name of God. What is gained from this wellspring of unending love may be given away as freely as it can be. There will always be more. It is a love that has itself been given freely to us, given without limit, given in a way that asks nothing of us but that we accept it—while also allowing us the freedom to reject it if we choose. But even such rejection does not stop its offer. It is a love that continues to be placed before us whether we choose to acknowledge it or not.

It is not always easy to accept a love so freely given. We assume that it cannot be truly meant for us. This too is something Brother Lawrence knew well. He writes:

I regard myself as the most wretched of all men, stinking and covered with sores, and as one who has committed all sorts of crimes against his

King. Overcome by remorse, I confess all my wickedness to Him, ask His pardon and abandon myself entirely to Him to do with as He wills. But this king, filled with goodness and mercy, far from chastising me, lovingly embraces me, makes me eat at His table, serves me with His own hands, gives me the keys of His treasures and treats me as His favorite. He talks with me and is delighted with me in a thousand and one ways.[21]

Too often we see ourselves as despicable. Behind the facade, the manners, the laughter, the stylish clothes we use to convince ourselves and others of the contrary, this is how we really feel. It is not in God's eyes that we appear this way, but in our own secret self-scrutiny. In God's eyes we are marvelous and wonderful. We delight God, as Brother Lawrence says, in a thousand and one ways. To accept God's love is to accept ourselves as lovable— lovable not for what we have done, not for what we say, not for how we act, but lovable deep down, for who we are. It takes time to convince ourselves of this. And it is for this reason that, for Brother Lawrence, living in the presence of the Lord requires *practice*. It takes practice for us to allow ourselves to see the beauty of who we are. We need help with this practice, and Brother Lawrence makes several suggestions. I have modified them and divided them into four points: (1) reflect before beginning each task; (2) repeat a short prayer as you work; (3) reflect after you finish each task; and (4) work at this reflection and prayer steadily with all jobs. These will be elaborated in the next chapter, but at this point it is important to understand what I am saying about these practices. None in any way attempts to bring us God's love.

We cannot effect our own salvation. These exercises are merely ways in which we come to feel the love that is already there. We do not somehow force God's love by praying; we only help ourselves to recognize the love that has always been held out to us all along.

To find this awareness of the presence of God in each moment of your life is to discover the secret of the sacred within the ordinary, which is the heart of the sacrament of the routine. It is, as I said, to know moments of great and unexpected joy. Brother Lawrence in fact confesses that it sometimes causes me interior, and often exterior happiness and joy so great that in order to moderate them and prevent their outward manifestation, I am obliged to resort to behavior that seems more foolishness than piety.[22]

But joy is only one of the gifts of this life. Another is that of consolation and courage. A mysterious strength and confidence—far greater than your own—comes with it. Then, too, you will find yourself more accepting of yourself and of others, since to discover that just as you are, you are loved, opens you to love others in the same way. And, finally, you may find that your faith itself has been transformed. For many people faith means nothing more than a set of beliefs to which they may either agree or disagree. To have faith is much like having an opinion, the only exception being that, where other opinions might concern politics or sports, this is an opinion on whether or not God exists. Living the presence of God, though, faith is transformed from an opinion to a relationship. God is not a belief to which you give your assent. God becomes a reality that you know intimately, meet every day, one whose strength becomes your strength, whose love, your love. Live this life of the presence of God long enough and when someone asks you, "Do you believe there is a God?" you may find yourself answering, "No, I do not *believe* there is a God. I *know* there is a God."

God is always present to us. The greatest thing we can do in life is to teach ourselves to be always present to God. The small, routine tasks that fill every day spent in the care of others may seem to be a barrier to this, but they need not. They may in fact be turned into one of the finest of spiritual disciplines, a special sacrament of the routine through which what to others appears the most ordinary and mundane of tasks is revealed to be a sacred act, an act of prayer. Prayer is nothing more or less than this, being present to God. And so this is a spirituality that makes all of life into prayer, a prayer of love, a prayer of help for others, a prayer of courage. It is a prayer that spans a lifetime, a prayer of great beauty.

8. Promoting the Spirituality of the Family

You are with us, Lord, but how seldom we know it. Open our eyes, open our hearts. Teach us to see and to feel that we are not alone, that you are with us in all we do, embracing us with your love and your care.

The spirituality of the family is made up of the sacrament of the care of others and the sacrament of the routine. What each involves has already been indicated, along with some of the ways in which they might be developed. But it might help to elaborate on the ways in which a man or a woman might find within the busy complexities of family life a means to spiritual discipline. There are three different ways to do this: turning activity inward, turning the inward into activity, and turning to others in celebration.

TURNING ACTIVITY INWARD

In the days when ships crossed the great oceans under sail, one of the most important instruments on board was something called a compass rose. A compass rose was a metal disk into which were etched layers of pointed petals indicating the four directions and their many subdivisions. The disk floated on a viscous solution within a metal casing so that no matter which direction the ship turned, the magnetized point of its northern petal would always be pointing north. The night might be completely overcast, with no stars visible to indicate position. The day might be so thick with fog that any reading from the sun was impossible. Currents might subtly shift the ship's direction, or fierce winds turn it completely about, but whatever happened, the compass rose would reveal the ship's direction. And if the ship were blown off course, it would be there silently pointing whenever the navigator went to consult it.

By turning inward we can each find our own compass rose, that part of the soul always pointing toward God. This is not quite what most people mean by conscience; it is deeper, purer—something never to be doubted but not found unless sought. We need to find this compass rose of the soul and, once found, consult it frequently. When we learn to set our course by it, it can show the way when everything seems confused, when everything is dark and uncertain. And when something occurs in life that completely turns us around, upsetting and disturbing everything so we no longer know which way to go, we can go inside ourselves to find this compass rose and there it will be, silently pointing the way to God.

I recommend three ways to turn inward. The author of *The Way of the Pilgrim* suggests repeating over and over the simple prayer, "Lord Jesus Christ, have mercy on me." Brother Lawrence also recommends the repetition of one short, simple prayer. The first two of my own recommendations are merely more detailed forms of these two suggestions, but although all three recommended methods are similar in some ways and different in others, they are complementary, so that they may either be practiced alone or along with the others.

My first suggestion, then, for turning activity inward is with a prayer of quiet. For this, take a few minutes alone in a room where you will not be disturbed. The morning is best, before beginning work. Other good times are at noon or in the early evening—or whenever you have a few moments to yourself. Take the phone off the hook; find a chair that is comfortable but not too comfortable. Close your eyes and take several slow, deep breaths to relax. Then slowly, without forcing it, begin to repeat a short prayer to yourself. Both the pilgrim and Brother Lawrence suggest prayers of only a few words. For this prayer of quiet, the shorter the prayer, the better. A single word is ideal. If, for example, you normally pray, "Lord Jesus Christ, have mercy on me," shorten it here simply to "Jesus." And if you usually pray, "Lord, I am with you," now just pray "Lord." Repeat your little prayer silently to yourself at whatever speed seems comfortable. Try repeating it each time you breathe in and again each time you breathe out. There is no need to try to think of anything or to do anything. It is best to let the word sweep away thoughts and images. To pray is to be present to the Lord. By praying this simple, powerful prayer you are as present as you can be. Just rest in God's presence. If you are disturbed or begin to think of other things, do not let it upset you. Just return to your prayer. And if there comes a time when even that one-word prayer seems unnecessary and you feel completely enveloped in God's care, then let the word go so that you rest in God's embrace in complete silence.

Nearly everyone finds this form of prayer difficult to begin. We are too accustomed to distraction. But continue this every day for at least twenty minutes a time, and over a period of several months you will find, first, that there will be days when the prayer is very easy, and—more than easy—it soon becomes wonderfully delightful. But even more amazing, you will find that whether or not the twenty minutes pass quickly or slowly, an enduring peacefulness will begin to follow you even into your most hectic hours.

A second suggestion for turning activity inward is to join prayer with work in the way Brother Lawrence suggests. As I said in the last chapter, I divided Brother Lawrence's recommendations into four points. These are:

1. *Reflect before beginning each task.* Before starting any job, stop a moment. It need not be for more than a second or so. Look inside yourself. Remind yourself that right at that moment you delight God in a thousand and one ways. Remind yourself that God loves you just as you, and that God has always loved you and always will. Try to feel this great love directed toward you, so that when you begin your work you make it a response to that love.

2. *Repeat a short prayer as you work.* It should be no more than five words, perhaps something like "Lord, I am with you." The shorter, the better. Just to say "Lord" or "Jesus" is enough. Prayer can draw you into the beauty of each passing moment by focusing your attention on the details of the task itself. Do not force the

prayer. Repeat it as you work, allowing it, perhaps, to follow the rhythm of your breathing. There may be times when the task requires greater concentration and you may have to set the prayer aside and times when it seems to slip away on its own. Let it go. There may also come a time when, without actually saying it to yourself, you seem to feel the prayer following the beat of your heart. All these are good. But as soon as you feel again that you are alone and hollow inside, begin the prayer once more.

3. *Reflect after you finish each task.* Again, this need not be more than a second or so. Simply look inward to who you are and see that you are loved. Consider the task you have just completed and offer it to God as your way of returning God's love, perhaps by saying to yourself, "This, Lord, is for you."

4. *Do not be discouraged, but work at reflection and prayer steadily with all jobs, large and small.*

These suggestions are simple enough, but that does not make them easier to keep up. Even doing them for one task will help draw you just that much closer to a realization of God's love. And every time you do them it gets easier and easier, because there begin to be periods when the full realization of who you are as a truly worthy and loved person bursts upon you with a sense of deep gratitude and happiness.

The third way to turn activity inward is less precise than the other two—it is to get into the habit of sharing thoughts and feelings with the Lord. This does not require special words or times alone, but it does require, first, that you learn to notice your feelings, hopes, and needs, and, second, that you are willing to speak of them to the Lord.

Our feelings draw us very close to who we are and by sharing them with the Lord, we are sharing ourselves. By bringing our feelings before God we are both discovering more of ourselves— our hidden selves—and learning to know the extent of God's love for us.

Sharing feelings with the Lord in this way is an act of prayer. It is a prayer that can come any time, but most especially when you are aware that the barometer of your moods has shifted. Begin to notice such moments. When you realize that you are feeling sadder than a moment before, or happier, or when you feel worried, or angry, or insulted, or put down, bring that to the Lord. Begin simply, "Lord, just now I feel . . ." and go on to silently explain *how* you feel in as much detail as you can. Examine also what might have caused you to feel the way you do, if you are at all aware of what that might be. Do this while you are working, if you are able, or take a few minutes when you have a chance to be alone later. As you examine your feelings, imagine Jesus beside you, listening with total understanding, not judging a single word you say but listening just because he wants to be with you. Be as honest as you can. Hold nothing back. No feeling can be condemned. If you feel angry, say so. If you feel hatred, say so. Only by being brought to the Lord in this way, can the positive strength behind every feeling be brought out, so that what otherwise might have been destructive and harmful is transformed into something life-giving. And after you have told the Lord what you can, ask the Lord about it. Deep within yourself you will hear the Lord's answer.

Each of these three forms of prayer, the prayer of quiet, the prayer of work, and the prayer of dialogue which brings your feelings to the Lord, is especially suited to drawing your activity inward. They each do three things. First, each makes the Lord's presence in your life into a reality of which you are always aware. Second, each shows you who you are, revealing your needs and your strengths in a way that inevitably leads you to that compass rose within your soul that points steadily, unwaveringly toward God, revealing the true course to take. Third, by discovering that God is present at every turn of the labyrinth of your personality, you will begin to appreciate the full extent of God's love for you. By finding that God is with you in your weakness, your doubt, your anger, and your loss, you will see that God can heal what needs to be healed and that God will never desert you.

These methods of prayer may be used alone or together. It is essential, however, to go into yourself one way or another and really discover the presence of God in your life. Without doing that, you are only going through the motions. But when you go inward, you will find a deep peacefulness accompanied by an energy that seems to flow into you from a source beyond yourself, an energy that fills all you do and draws you forward to reach out to others—an energy that asks you to turn the inward into activity.

TURNING THE INWARD INTO ACTIVITY

As you discover the power and fullness of God's presence within you, your activities will be transformed of themselves. But since this is something that may occur over many years, you may help the process by reminding yourself consciously of three truths that may at first be hard to accept but will eventually appear so obvious that they hardly need to be expressed at all.

The first of these is that an action is judged great according to the love with which it is performed and by nothing else. The movements of nations, the construction of buildings, the formation of public policy—these may be done for power, expediency, personal gain, or even for the general good. If not done for love, they are nothing. But do even the smallest thing out of love—crouch down to listen patiently to a child tugging on your coat, urgently wanting to tell you something he has discovered, or carefully shape dough into loaves and watch to see that they bake as long as they should but no longer—do things like this with love and the love within the act will become a seed planted, unseen and unsuspected, in the hearts of others, a seed that grows in secret so that it may be years or even decades before the flower of this seed is revealed. From that one act of love others will come, extending and growing, the circle stretching wider and wider through the centuries.

The second of these truths is that any work done for love is an act of worship. It becomes a special devotion, a prayer. And recognized as this, it must be seen as something that requires total attention, with full care given to every detail. Attentiveness to the work being done is a spiritual virtue. It is not right to see some things—creative tasks or prayer, for example—as superior to others. Any task can become an act of devotion, just as any may be falsely glorified. All deserve equal care.

The final truth follows from this last. Since all that we do becomes an act of devotion, each person's life becomes one long litany of praise. Each life is unique. Each life expresses in a different way the same truth at the center of all that is. Each of us is the principal celebrant at a special celebration of the incarnation, one that continues for our full lifetime. It is up to us to make the celebration as beautiful as possible.

Seeing all of life as a celebration of the divine mystery, it is natural that we should want to make that celebration explicit from time to time. And this too is a way to promote the spirituality of the family.

TURNING TO OTHERS IN CELEBRATION

Church provides an opportunity for worship within the wider community. As important as this is, those wishing to promote family life as a spiritual discipline should also look for ways in which short worship services can be brought into the home. The earliest Christian services were in homes. Several families and friends would gather to pray and share a meal together. The bread and wine consecrated for the Eucharist was taken from the bread and wine that would be their meal immediately after the prayers. It was really the size of the growing Christian community that made it necessary to move the gathering to a building set aside for worship services and to separate the Eucharist from an actual meal.

The spirituality of the family can be deepened by finding ways of worshiping within the home. But that requires searching out symbols that epitomize life at the center and reviving models Christianity has forgotten. Judaism has a long tradition of home worship. Passover—the commemoration Jesus altered in a way that would become the Eucharist—is celebrated during a family meal, as is also that set of readings, blessings, and prayers used to inaugurate the Sabbath.

In Boston's South End there is a place called Haley House, which offers meals to the homeless of the city as well as for the elderly of the neighborhood and beds to those who need a place to stay. Haley House is a Catholic Worker House, inspired by the one first started in the 1930s by Dorothy Day to bring Jesus's love and care directly to those who need it. Although it is Catholic, those who live there and help out are from a variety of faiths—Catholic, Protestant, Quaker, Jewish—and they work to find ways to express all faiths.

Occasionally my wife, Pamela, and I and our three children go to Haley House to help them prepare the evening meal for the elderly. If there are enough people to help, everyone eats together, servers and served alike, otherwise those who cook and wash eat later. Friday night, however, is always set aside as a time for those who live at Haley House and their guests to eat together. One Friday we joined them and saw why. On Friday they celebrate together the coming of the Sabbath.

We sat around the table. The Sabbath candles, candles that would burn during the meal that night, were blessed and lit. One of the older children read a psalm. A cup of wine was blessed and passed hand to hand, person to person as everyone took a sip. Another psalm was read. Then the bread was blessed and it too was passed so that everyone could take it, break off a piece, then pass it along. There was a final prayer and the meal began.

A glow lingered as we ate. We were just a small group, but as we talked and laughed together and discussed what had been happening that day, we felt ourselves tied to something larger. The food and drink before us, the candles that gave us light, the company of friends and family, the evening itself as well as the day that preceded it and the day that was to follow it—all this was joined into a long peaceful moment which, even as we experienced it for all it was, also joined us to the past and to the future in ways we could not ignore.

The Sabbath begins Friday evening at sunset and continues until sunset on Saturday. It is the seventh day which, according to

Genesis, was the day when God rested. In Judaism it is a day set apart from the rest of the week as a time to remember and be thankful for God's creation. In setting aside this one day and marking with prayers, readings, and blessings its beginning on Friday evening and its ending on Saturday evening, the day becomes a time to remember again that God is always present and that it is through God's love for us that we seek to love and care for each other. It is a time to renew the understanding of the truths that are the basis of the spirituality of the family.

I have shortened and adapted the Jewish service of the Inauguration of the Sabbath. It, along with several other services for home worship, is appended to this book. The service does not take more than ten minutes and can be done as the family sits around the table immediately before the Friday evening meal. Because it is a family worship, everyone in the family should participate. Husband and wife should alternate the different blessings and prayers. The psalms are set up so that the first verse is read by one person, the second by everyone, the third by that person again, and so on. Children in the early grades seem to be particularly pleased to be the main readers of these psalms. The service is brief, but it can become something to which all, even children, look forward, sensing as even they do the mysterious way it reminds them that right then and there they participate in the eternal.

This Jewish service has special value to Christians because these are the very prayers and blessings of candles, bread, and wine that Jesus himself used to welcome the Sabbath, but there are many other forms that home worship might take. It helps to experiment with different forms. There are a few things, however, to consider when thinking about home worship:

1. Keep it short and simple. This is especially important if there are small children. If there are several children below the age of five, the service should be very short indeed and made up of no more than a few simple acts such as the passing and the breaking of bread.

2. Find a way for as many as possible to take part. The whole point of family worship is to make all conscious of how much everyone in the family is touched by God's love and presence.

This comes through most clearly when all are able to participate as fully as possible in the service. It is also much more fun that way. Parents should alternate prayers and blessings between themselves. Children old enough to read should be encouraged to participate in that way. Smaller children should be given some small task to perform.

3. Do not rely only on words; find simple symbolic gestures to represent the important parts of family life. Spoken prayers or psalms alone quickly become boring to children and there is the risk that adults as well as children may come to see faith as something abstract and distant. Rather, bring in the common gestures of your life together; incorporate into worship the regular actions of the day. Meals are one of the important family activities and to worship just before a meal, using candles, bread, and wine as principal symbols, is particularly evocative, but there are other important acts of the day that can be marked in family worship. Anyone with small children knows how important those moments just before bedtime can be. These offer an excellent opportunity for a period of sharing with a toddler. After reading the child a story, tell the child that it is time to worship together. Then, sing a song together. Children love to sing. If the child uses a night light, you could use that as the central symbol. After the song, ask the child if there is anything he or she wants to thank God for, after which you pray, saying at the end while switching on the night light, "This night light will be on all night; in the same way God will be with you all night."

4. Come to recognize the power of repetition. There is no need to come up with different forms of worship or to change from week to week. The same words and actions said from one week to the next do not grow stale but begin to take on levels of significance not first noticed. The whole service becomes more and more evocative as it is repeated over and over. Children sense this even more than adults. Children are deeply reassured by repetition. It suggests to them continuity and connection.

5. Invite others to join you. Home worship, especially that centering around a meal, is something to share with relatives and

friends. It can add new dimensions to the friendship just as it adds new dimensions to faith.

6. Have fun. Do not equate worship with being solemn. Relax and enjoy whatever small changes may occur spontaneously in service.

One final word about worship at home. It is not meant to be in any way a substitute for worship with a wider community at church. It is instead something that can enhance and deepen that other worship, giving all family members a fuller sense of their own personal connection to God and to others, which will make participation in a larger worshiping community even more meaningful.

Turning activity inward, turning the inward into activity, turning to others in celebration—these are three ways to live family life as a spiritual discipline. And that it is a discipline make no mistake. No hermit in the desert ever had one harder. But live out these three principles and the life of the family will be revealed to be one truly lived at the center. Its meaning will be clear, its gifts obvious.

9. The Gifts of the Spirituality of the Family

Jesus, most of your life you spent in Nazareth as co-worker, neighbor, and friend to those around you. The special gifts of your life, hidden to history, are revealed each day within the lives of those who live, as you did, at the center. Teach me to see these gifts; teach me to value what is at once so ordinary and so precious so that I too can come to know you as co-worker, as neighbor, and as friend.

The gifts of the spirituality of the family are many, but they are only slowly revealed. Living this life a person finds a completeness, a fullness, but a fullness that grows so subtly it is seldom noticed for the great gifts it contains.

First, there is the gift of caring for others. This is gift and discipline, both. As difficult and demanding as care can be, it is something all of us long to give. It is strange that, with all the importance we place on meeting all our other needs, we so often ignore this one. It is passed over as if it were not a true need at all. But look closer, look at the vast numbers of people suffering acutely from the pain of loneliness. Is it really that they are so alone? Not at all. These people have colleagues, they have relatives, they have friends. Still they feel lonely because there is no one among that group who needs their care. That terrible, empty feeling we call loneliness is nothing other than the feeling that comes when there is no one to take care of.

No matter how crowded with people a life is, with no one to take care of a person feels empty, something meaningful has been removed. I have yet to meet a person who was able to work at a job for even one day unless she or he could believe that there was at least one other person in the world who would benefit from what was being done. To come to believe that the work is no help to anyone is to feel it suddenly robbed of all meaning. This is how closely meaning is linked to the care of others.

This powerful craving of the soul to care for others is in its own way as insistent and important as the needs of the body. A person can live weeks without food, days without water, and minutes without air, but deny each long enough and death is inevitable. How long can a person go without ever meeting the need to care for another human being? Perhaps there might be some who could hobble through a lifetime, numb to the dull ache of loneliness and the hollowness of life without meaning, but the toll would be overwhelming. Nearly everyone recognizes in some part of their being the care of others to be the wonderful gift it is. Deny its calling and a person suffers great loss. Answer it and know the satisfaction of that rich inner warmth that is opposite of loneliness; answer it and know also that sense of purpose and direction that is the opposite of meaninglessness.

A second gift of the spirituality of the family is the experience of the vulnerability of love. Too often we try to protect ourselves by closing ourselves off. We build walls around ourselves, turn the soul into a fortress and raise the drawbridge. If no one can come near to us, we seem to believe, then no one can hurt us. But such fortresses are always cramped, insular spaces. To lock yourself inside is to place yourself within a prison, a place where you slowly decay while suffering from a thousand imagined hurts. It is far better to tear down the walls, to take the risk of meeting people and having them meet you, to stand unprotected.

A seed can never grow until it first bursts the shell around it. A bird will never fly until it hatches from its egg. And when we retreat into some hidden corner of ourselves, we are not really making ourselves more safe, only trapping ourselves within a thin shell that keeps us from becoming all we might become. To break out *is* at first to be vulnerable. A shoot first breaking through the soil *is* something tender and easily hurt. A baby bird newly hatched *is* awkward and unsure. But to take that risk and continue is the only way the small shoot will ever grow into a powerful tree, the only way the bird will ever have a chance to soar. And it is only by breaking out of the shell of self-protection that a person can become that magnificent sort of human being that can give and receive love with spontaneity and warmth.

The family has been the place where many have learned to do this. To commit yourself to another in marriage—committing yourself for a future that contains nothing but uncertainty—is to begin to break out of the shell. To take on the responsibility of the care of children, with all that that demands, is to free yourself from it still more. And to continue with this day after day, and renew commitment in the face of difficulty, accept responsibility in the face of heavy demands, is to slowly begin to come into your own and to grow into who you are.

A third gift of the spirituality of the family is the center of trust it can provide, a trust that can become the foundation to challenge the distrust of the world. It is a trust that comes of knowing that there is a place where you might go when you need to be held, but that you will not be held back when you need to go forth. Such a place the family can be and to know that it is there is deeply reassuring. It can be the basis of a strength to stand against the cruelty that the world inflicts. It also can be a silent witness against the fear and hostility that is so rampant now, offering another way.

A fourth gift is the chance to live the greatest of all rituals, one that moves along to celebrate the intimate details of the human seasons. It is a ritual that passes the point at which life is transformed into prayer. The first three gifts of the spirituality of the family—care, love, and trust—are those that come from reaching out to those nearest to you and into the world beyond. But it is at this point that the gifts are all transformed, so that you come to feel the world reaching out to you in turn, but not the world as an abstraction. Better rather to say that you come to sense some powerful force at the center of all that is, a force at once infinite in majesty, while also small and intimate—vaster than the universe itself and as close to you as the beating of your own heart. To come to know this is to come to know those earlier gifts on another level entirely. It is to know a care for us far beyond the care we can give to others, to know a love for us willing to become so vulnerable as to suffer death for our sake, and to know a trust for who we are that even as that love holds us, nurtures us, it also leaves us free to become whatever we determine we must become —even if that involves turning from the love and rejecting the care. It is to know that no matter how avidly we might reach out to embrace the world and all it contains, there is an infinitely powerful, infinitely loving force reaching out to embrace us more avidly still. It is to know that God is Love.

III. CHILDCARE IN THE DESERT—DRAWING THE TWO WAYS OF LIFE TOGETHER

10. The Family Alone

Lord, you made each of us a marvel of creation, at once unique and eternal. Help us to draw out both the talents that are uniquely our own and that love and care for others that knows no end. Both are from you, both for you. And in both together we become complete. Give us, Lord, the strength, the wisdom, and the courage each requires.

The spirituality of life at the center is complete in itself. It is a spiritual discipline to which nothing need be added. Through the sacrament of the care of others a person, by reaching within to find a love to give away, finds in addition a love meant especially for him or for her alone; through the sacrament of the routine a person comes to discover the profound meaning that comes when life itself is turned into prayer. Felt first simply as two separate spiritual needs—the need to care for another and the need to find the meaning, the sacredness, within the ordinary—if sought persistently and conscientiously they become together the means to break through into new revelation.

There is nothing that *need* be added to this spirituality, but there is something that many may *want* to add to it, for in addition to the need to discover love through the care of others and the need to find the meaning within the ordinary, there is the need to investigate and express personal uniqueness. This is the need the spirituality of the desert pursues. By going into the barren wilderness to pray alone in a cave, those early Christians who first adopted the desert as their home were consciously setting themselves apart from other men and women, creating a manner of worship unique to each of them and separate from all others, one that sought solitude to provide a contact with God that was again unique, a relationship quite unlike any other.

These days, the spiritual impulse that drove people to the harsh loneliness of the desert can be recognized in many less extreme forms. It can be seen in any desire for creative expression and, in fact, in any yearning to develop those talents—artistic, educational, business—that are uniquely your own.

Many, of course, see this as nothing other than self-advancement. It can be that. Public recognition may come to some who develop themselves in this way, and so the longing may become nothing other than the fuel to feed ambition. But the true need is for something deeper than recognition or esteem and persists whether it gains the person the attention of others or not. It is a craving to develop those separate talents with which each of us is born, a craving that is really quite independent of the inclination some may have to imagine themselves famous and admired.

Each person born has a combination of strengths and gifts that are duplicated by no one who has ever been or is ever yet to be. Each of us senses this, although sometimes in ways only in small part conscious. And just as a child, born with all the muscles, as yet undeveloped, that will allow her to walk, will on her own find ways to strengthen those muscles—crawling at first, then surprising her parents by using the leg of a chair to pull herself up so that she stands, holding the chair as she, wobbling uncertainly, works to steady herself, then eventually taking those first steps across the room—just as this child has an innate impulse to cultivate and develop the physical capacity she shares with all human beings, so will she have, as she grows older, a mounting desire to discover and cultivate those skills she does not share, those skills that are uniquely her own.

Each of us is wondrously made. At every birth there is a new genesis where all seven days of creation are blended into one, so that from the particles of energy that are the stuff of the universe a new being is formed. This new being is the product of the final day of creation; it contains a bit of every one that preceded it but also contains something more, which had not been offered by God to the world until that day—the ability for creation itself. Kneaded into the very substance of our flesh is the dim, inarticulate memory of words whispered into our ears long before they were capable of hearing any words but God's. "Continue my creation,"

God said to each of us as every bone and sinew listened. "It is I who began the work and made you, but it is you who must finish the work and make yourself complete. Do *this* work, and you do *my* work."

We alone of all God made were given the gift of self-creation. We crave the chance to use this gift, so powerful and so wonderful. We crave the opportunity to find what we are good at doing; to learn, to practice, to show what we can do. We look for ways to flex and strengthen the muscles of those talents we suspect, or hope, or come at times to doubt we have. And such self-creation can become a magnificent hymn of praise to God.

Although the need for self-creation has driven some into the desert, it is not so much where or how this life is lived as what it aims to achieve that makes it inevitable that this be a life lived on the edge. A person who is working to form herself into all that she can be must in some way set herself apart from the rest of humanity. Even if she does not go into the desert, she must see herself as separate and be willing to make choices based on this understanding, because self-creation requires that there be time alone, that whatever need be done for fulfillment *is* done, and that self-creation alone remain the principal preoccupation.

And yet, as pointed out many times already, such a preoccupation is not readily compatible with those other preoccupations that form the life at the center. The orientation toward those who need care, joined with the persistence and regularity of the work that must be done to make this care possible, seems to leave little opportunity for the solitude, the separation, and the self-formation that is the basis of life on the edge. Life at the center is one that lives great truths, but it does not allow for *this*. Life at the center works to maintain stability; it is steady, regular. It has its schedule of things that must be done, and the interruptions it knows are those that others make. Life on the edge is one that is willing to take risks. It does not place high on its list of priorities the stability that regular care expects and so cannot easily maintain the sort of schedule a family needs. It breaks away from the standard and the routine.

For those who feel the craving for self-creation most acutely, the greatest frustration of a life lived for the care of others is the sense that something crying out for recognition has been stifled, forced to remain trapped within them day after day, year after year. On the other hand, life on the edge, if pursued with single-minded purpose, seldom provides the opportunity for those profoundly intimate relationships of marriage and parenthood which, when denied long enough, can leave a person, no matter what he or she might otherwise have accomplished, feeling a hollow ache of emptiness.

There are many of us who cannot be satisfied abandoning either of these options. We feel the need for the self-enrichment that life on the edge allows; we feel the need to care for others and to live within the beauty of everyday tasks that life at the center makes possible. Although either way of life has riches enough for anyone, there are some of us for whom neither alone is quite enough, for whom the question raised earlier and then postponed has persisted: can these two ways of life be joined?

It is a question that elicits two responses, both equally important. The first response is yes, the two ways of life *can* be joined. The second response is that the difficulty of doing this should not be underestimated. Only in both responses together is the complete answer to be found. It is a deception to say glibly that yes, of course, they can be joined and minimize the difficulty this involves. It is an equal deception to stress the difficulties so much that the option no longer seems possible. And yet the fact is that different groups at different times in the history of Christianity tended to do just this, point to one half of the answer or to the other and imply either that the joining of these two ways of life could be done with little problem at all or else that it was a project that was all but impossible.

Protestants and Catholics have traditionally emphasized different halves of the answer. Catholics have most frequently assumed that the two ways of life were impossible to join and so required that priests and other religious—monks and nuns—accept celebacy as a prerequisite to this life on the edge. Anyone who looks closely into the matter will see that the contemporary arguments in defense of celebacy have far less to do with the notion that sexuality is impure and so must be denied to those who seek a life of fullest sanctity, as they do with the belief that the demands of spouse and children are just so great that they cannot be fit with the separate preoccupations of life on the edge. The life of complete spiritual fulfillment is reserved for those who will never marry. To everyone else remains the exclusive option of the spirituality of the life of the family, a life only imperfectly recognized as one offering a kind of spirituality at all.

Both groups have suffered from this separation. The laity have suffered from feelings of inferiority, from a sense that their way of life was somehow not as spiritual as that of priests, monks, and nuns, that they were prisoners of a life of routine that barred them from the possibility of fullest spiritual enrichment. Priests and religious, on the other hand, have often suffered from the isolation and impoverishment of personality that comes from a life denied the deepest forms of intimacy. Deciding that the spirituality of the edge and that of the center could not be joined resulted in a church divided into two main groups, those allowed to marry and those choosing celebacy. This has made the church easier to regulate, but at a terrible price to all.

On the other hand, there can be equally disastrous results in assuming, as Protestants often do, that the two may be joined with no difficulty at all. The separation between a life lived for self-development, either through a rewarding career, a creative enterprise, or a life of radical discipleship, and that of steady care for a family is for many denominations assumed to be an artificial one. Both ways of life are attempted at once. But with no special provisions made to see that one does not dominate, a pattern frequently develops where one person, most often the wife, is relegated to a position where care of the family becomes her only option, while the other, usually the husband, takes a role where the family becomes for him little more than a stopping-off point, a place for him to pause whenever the demands of his career make it convenient.

In not recognizing the difficulties of joining the two ways of life, the separation returns once more in unacknowledged ways, forming a schism within the family itself. On the one side is the wife. She may have preferred to give most of her time to the care of home and children, but she did not expect to be so denied *all* opportunity for self-development, that while her husband engaged in exciting and stimulating activity she would continually be left to hold her peace and wait. On the other side is the husband. He may have assumed that his career would be the main source of income for the family, but he never expected that it would result in an emotional celebacy where so much of family life was denied him that he would come to feel almost a stranger in his home, recognizing all the furnishings and the decorations, but not recognizing those who share the rooms with him. Neither partner expected or wanted this, and neither saw it developing in the first years of marriage. And yet all at once there it was. The effort needed to truly join into the fullness of one life these separate lives was not anticipated.

Whenever a person accepts two separate sets of responsibilities, there eventually comes a time when he or she will have to choose between them, and it is human nature to choose consistently one way or the other—desert or family. This is even true for those whose particular "desert" involves the care of others. There are children of more ministers than one who tell stories of the many times when they were lonely or needed help or advice, only to discover that their father did not have time for them because he had to provide instead company, help, or advice for one of his parishioners. The family within a parish least often ministered to is the family of the minister himself.

In bringing the two ways of life together, five important rules must be practiced. They do not make the job easy, but they do make it possible. The benefits of joining the two make the effort worthwhile. These five rules are: balance time, arrange space, keep close, perform rituals of separation and return, and, finally, learn to live off balance.

BALANCING TIME

Lack of time is of course the central problem. The life of care of others is one that consumes every moment of the day. How is it possible to find more time for the self-creation of life on the edge? The answer is that it is not possible to find *more* time, but it is possible to find *some* time. In any busy schedule there is some time that can be set aside for whatever your need for self-creation most demands—prayer, reading, outside work. But you must consciously set aside for one period every day. Try to make as few exceptions as possible. Have a prearranged minimum length for it (it may be as little as twenty minutes) in a period of the day when you are least likely to be disturbed and most able to make good use of the time. It may be in the morning before work begins, or during a child's nap time, or during a lunch break, or in the early evening.

Whenever it is, whatever its length, stick to it. Make whatever arrangements have to be made to limit disturbances. If at home, take the phone off the hook. If the time is to be taken during a lunch break at work, let your co-workers know that, although you enjoy their company, you really want a few moments to yourself for part of the hour. Think of the time as special. Honor the commitment involved.

Periods of caring for others should be interwoven, then, with strictly adhered to, prearranged periods of withdrawal. In the same way, times spent in activities away from the family should be followed with times together with the family. For those who spend most of their time outside the home and are likely to be together with spouse and children for only brief periods, more is needed than just a few hours of physical presence in the evening. A family develops a life of its own. Someone absent from the family for most of the hours the family is together may find that he or she no longer has a place in the events that are occurring—unless that person actively works at engaging with the family when they are together. You do not have to create special activities. Time spent holding a small child or reading him a story at night, time spent talking with an older child or helping with homework, time spent making the dinner an opportunity for everyone to share each other's company, time spent talking with one's spouse in the evening about the incidents of the day and the plans for the days and weeks ahead—these are the moments that balance time spent away from the family.

These are balances to try for from day to day, but there is another sort of balance too, a balance maintained throughout a lifetime. Every life has many phases, many cycles. A person who must follow the wishes of her parents as a child may find greater freedom as a young adult, followed by a period when she is controlled once more by the demands of children or of the early stages of a career, followed again by a period of freedom as the children grow more independent or her career reaches that point when she, not others, is in control. This may be followed by another kind of dependence. The cycle continues. It goes back and forth. Nothing remains as it was.

An elderly lady approaches a young mother. She stops to admire the baby, then, asking permission, takes the baby in her arms, hugs him, and cradles him.

"Enjoy him while you can," she says as she hands the baby back. "He will be grown before you know it."

The mother nods vaguely. Perhaps the elderly lady has not seen the fatigue her eyes express or the discouragement she feels because so much that she wants to get done is not getting done. Perhaps she did not notice the hint of tolerant skepticism that passed briefly over her face as if to say, "This pass? You don't know what you're saying. I'm locked in." Perhaps she did not see this, but then again perhaps she did, and it was for that very reason she chose to speak.

The fact is that times of intense care *do* pass. In retrospect they *do* seem astonishingly brief. There may be periods, then, when the time available for self-creation may be at an absolute minimum, perhaps not available at all. These times will end. And although it is important that a person try as much as possible to work at maintaining some moments of private time even within the most demanding periods of care for others, there is a natural tendency of family life eventually to correct an imbalance and make more time available. Anticipate and prepare for this.

ARRANGING SPACE

The major difficulty in joining the life at the center with that on the edge is finding time for each, but a separate space for each is important too. Space is important to life at the center. The home is the focus of all family activities, much as it can become the focus of the family's awareness so that all the world is understood in relation to that one spot on the earth. The home is the center of care, and while we are at home the activities of that care seem to have a special compulsion. There are always things to be done. There are always interruptions. They are hard to ignore even during those times when no one else is home.

Everyone trying to join the life of self-creation with that of care needs a space all their own within the home, one set apart as much as possible, a place to withdraw. For those lucky enough, this might be a separate room all their own. For others it might be a desk they alone use or perhaps only a comfortable chair in a quiet corner of the bedroom.

Whatever form the space takes, it should be as much as possible something that is separate, that is your own, and that is used specifically for your private times away from the family. It should be first of all, then, as separate as possible. If the space is an extra room, that's no problem. If it is a desk or chair, it should be set in as private a place as can be found, one where there are least likely to be any disturbances. Second, it should be yours alone. A little possessiveness here is absolutely essential. So much of the life of the family is spent in sharing. This is meant to be a balance to that. Your special space should *not* be shared. A spouse should respect it and children be taught to honor it. Third, it must be recognized as a place to be used specifically as something apart from the family. In other words, *you* must honor it too. It is a place for what is important to you—reading, study, work, prayer, quiet withdrawal—and it should be used for that purpose alone.

Those who spend much of the day outside the home also need

such space. The home is the center; it is where the life of care takes place. An effort should be made to bring a bit of the spirituality of the desert into the home. Only then will you have the strength to take the love and care of the family outside the home to give to the wider world.

KEEPING CLOSE

Balancing time and arranging space are two ways to fit something of the life of the desert into that of the family. The more successfully you do these first two, the more important this third rule becomes, because it is this effort that seeks to ensure that nothing of the caring, the intimacy, and the sharing so essential to family life is lost.

Keeping close is simply that process of making the extra effort to reach out to those whose life you share. Sharing the same rooms and seeing each other day after day does not in itself draw people together. A bit too frequently it happens that a certain shallowness and superficiality slip into the relationships of family members. Children may grow into strangers to their parents, parents to their children. Husbands and wives may drift apart so slowly and in ways so small that neither really notices until they too are all but strangers. This has always been a danger in family life, one people have to work to prevent, but it is something those seeking to join the life of the family with that of the desert should particularly seek to avoid.

Activities for keeping close to children need not involve anything special or elaborate. The main thing is that children be aware that you are taking some of your time to spend especially with them. With smaller children this can be time spent playing or reading stories. Children seven years old to eleven or twelve particularly enjoy sharing discoveries with their parents; they like the chance to explain in detail and are flattered whenever a parent takes the time to hear their elaborate account of something learned in science or their detailed description of a movie. The focus of those in their early teens is on their friends. Their loyalties may have shifted enough that they may not share as freely as before, but if they sense true interest and openness from their parents, they are usually delighted to talk about the new relationships they find so exhilarating and so perplexing.

For husband and wife, keeping close is essential. The intimacy and closeness with which the marriage began will not continue on its own inertia. That intimacy was not formed spontaneously; it was something both partners actively worked to create. It is easy for those of us who have been married for a while to forget how much time and effort we spent to be someone special to that person we came to marry. There were the calls on the phone, the arrangements to meet as frequently as possible, the extra care in dressing when the two of us were to be together, the dinners that went long past the dinner hour, the shared walks, the little presents and the notes left for the other to find. It was all great fun, but it was also a special effort. The intimacy that led to marriage was something carefully built.

This effort should continue. It is particularly important that there be a time every day when a husband and wife can spend time just talking casually together without feeling the pressure of all they have to do. For some, this time might be found by getting up half an hour earlier in the morning to share a cup of coffee before the children awake and the day's work begins. For others, it might be easier to take time in the evening; perhaps once a week this daily time together could become a late dinner where, the children fed and either in bed or on their own, it is possible to spend a little extra time talking quietly by candlelight. Dates should continue. Small gifts and flowers are also ways to retain that feeling of first romance, that feeling of being special.

The more busy husband and wife become, the more care such things as these should be given. Being busy is no excuse for slowing down the romance within a marriage; it is the warning signal that it must be pursued all the more aggressively. If it becomes absolutely impossible to have time together every day, then find other means to keep close. Short notes left for each other to find, perhaps saying nothing more than "I love you, thank you for yesterday," or that you are looking forward to the time you will spend together in a day or so—these are the gestures that keep the ties strong. And when the separation is going to be longer than a day, or when both of you are so busy that you have not talked for a long while, consider writing short letters to each other—love letters—no more than a few sentences, to be mailed home or to where the other works. There in the pile of bills and junk mail your husband or wife will find a letter addressed with a familiar handwriting and open it to read, during this time of day when his or her thoughts might be on much different things, how much you mean to each other.

RITUALS OF SEPARATION AND RETURN

A ritual is a prescribed action. At its worst, ritual is the empty repetition of things done for no other reason than that they were always done. At its best, ritual becomes something that reveals the wider connections of life and expresses, through gesture and symbol, beliefs and feelings for which words alone are not enough.

The rituals most of us enact are done so routinely as to be almost unconscious, but there was a time in our culture, and still is in some other cultures, when daily life was rich with small rituals that reminded people of their connection with God and with those around them. The power of ritual needs to be rediscovered. As the repetition of actions it is particularly suited to incorporation within the life of the family, where so many activities are repeated again and again. And it may be with the small rituals that families working to join the spiritualities of the edge and at the center may give a new dimension to efforts to keep close while going their separate ways.

For many, the word "ritual" conjures up images of elaborate ceremonies, of incense and music. I am thinking of something much simpler, little gestures really, but gestures that come to remind family members of their ties to one another and that point to their efforts to stay close to one another even in situations where they may have to be separated for brief periods.

My wife, Pamela, and I have a small ritual of this sort which evolved by chance. The two of us met while studying in Japan. We were married in Tokyo and it was soon after that, while traveling through the southern island of Kyushu, that we visited a small, family-run pottery factory. The old grandfather designed vases, cups, and bowls on a pottery wheel. Those he liked would be used to form molds from which many more would be made. After talking with the family and watching them work we were shown a display of their complete line, a large case containing an example of every one of their current designs. All were beautiful, but there was one piece, a cup, which both Pamela and I immediately noticed. We both liked it. We asked if we could buy the set.

"Which one is it?" the young woman who was showing us the display asked in Japanese.

"This one over here."

"Oh I'm sorry," she said. "We no longer make that one. We should have removed it from the display. It is the last one we have."

She opened the case and took it out.

"Here," she said. "Please accept it as a gift."

Later we tried to decide what we were to do with this single cup. It seemed too lovely to use just as we would an odd mug, and yet since we only had one there would be no chance to use it with guests or even among ourselves.

"I know," Pamela said. "Let's make it a waiting cup. It will be the cup each of us uses only when the other is away. We'll use it while we wait for the other to return."

It has been that ever since. It may sit on the shelf unused for weeks or for months, but when one of us is forced to go on a trip without the other, the waiting cup is taken out. It is used for coffee in the morning and tea in the afternoon. It is used as long as the other is gone. With the return, it is put away.

It is a small gesture, but far more powerful and evocative than its simplicity would suggest. During those times when it was my turn to use the waiting cup, I would hold it and its color and unusual shape would draw from me a poignant sense of waiting, of suspension, which, mingling with the memories of the time the cup was given us and of some of the many things that have happened since, was both melancholy and somehow reassuring. With this simple gesture, our separations are fit within the larger context of connection.

Another way to mark separations of a day or longer is the lighting of a candle at the dinner table for every night someone is away; the flame symbolizes for the family that the missing one is with them in spirit. A little ritual of separation and return that small children especially enjoy is the exchanging of small personal items to be safeguarded during an absence. A child might give a small toy or a stone she found, the parent a tie clip or ribbon. Each keeps what he or she was given until the parent returns; then they give them back again.

Our society respects the precise meaning words can give but has largely forgotten the strata of meaning ritual can convey. Families especially must rediscover this. Its varied levels of association are ideally suited to reinforcing the family's varied levels of connection, especially the connections that must know the strain of joining the life of the family with that of the desert.

LIVING OFF BALANCE

The final rule for joining of the life of the desert with that of the family is remembering that the union is seldom a smooth one. The most turbulent places in the immense body of water that surrounds our planet are those spots where the great oceans meet. It is in places like Cape Horn, where the Atlantic and the Pacific meet, and where their separate heights, separate currents, and separate air streams flow into one another, that produce water notoriously treacherous to navigate. Bringing together these two ways of life, with their separate needs and expectations, can create similar turmoil.

Trying to join these lives produces a sense of perpetual imbalance. You work all morning to catch up on all that has to be done in order to get a little time to yourself, and, taking a few minutes, return renewed, only to be once more overwhelmed with countless interruptions and demands. You come home from work exhausted, drained, but somehow you must find the strength to spend some quality time with spouse and children. You work to meet the needs of those you care for as well as your own needs for self-creation. Often it seems much easier just to abandon one set of needs or the other, to turn away from the needs of your family or suppress your own desire for self-creation. But somehow you sense that either way something profound would be lost to you. So you continue, back and forth, never feeling that either task is really successful—that your care for those around you suffers because of your efforts at self-creation and self-creation suffers because of care for family.

The sensation is like trying to stand still and walk at the same moment. It is impossible to do both at once so you do a little of one, then a little of the other. You stand for a moment, then decide to walk, take a few steps, stop abruptly and stand again, then begin to walk once more. It is a halting, uneven, stumbling way to live, one where you feel always about to fall.

Life on the edge, life at the center—self-discovery, comfort for a child; quiet time alone, trying to find out why your husband seems so upset; finishing up the work that must be ready for a meeting tomorrow morning, washing the dinner dishes—back and forth it goes, a step, then a pause, a step, then a pause. You feel yourself an inhabitant of two worlds, but a citizen of neither. You feel always off balance.

And yet this sense of imbalance is part of the solution, not part of the problem, of joining the two ways of life. After all, you *are* living both. They *have* been brought together and the fact that they do not fit comfortably need not be taken as evidence of failure, but of the health of the struggle that refuses to let either one go.

The task now is to learn to accept this imbalance, to see in it a sign of all that is being attempted. And perhaps with practice there may come a time when the imbalance can be steadied, the halting, stumbling gait smoothed and evenly paced and so transformed into dance, a lifelong of dance that makes a home for a family and a place in the desert.

11. Family and Community

Dear God, help us to tear down the walls between people. Help us to replace distrust with openness, separation with sharing, fear with love. It is you who becomes the bond that connects people. Teach us to know you enough to seek that connection. Save us, God, from isolation.

It is possible to join the life of the desert with that of the family, but it is not easy. To return to an earlier image, the spirituality of the desert and that of the family are like two parts of a wheel. The first is the edge of the wheel. The life it offers is one of exhilaration and speed, but also one at times grinding, hard, and bitter. To give full expression to the longing for the desert is to risk the destruction that comes when reaching to the very border of human existence in the hope of touching the truly magnificent, all-powerful God. The spirituality of the family is the wheel's center. Slower and duller, it is also close to the core of things. To choose this life of caring is to accept the monotony of small demands, which can take up a lifetime as easily as they take up a day, in order to become part of the steady rhythm of the eternal.

But what about the spokes joining the edge and center of the wheel? In a family, husband and wife can work together to become those spokes. With their effort, the two can be joined, but a lot will then depend on each of them. There will be strain at times, and the links will not be as strong as either would probably like. But, then, two spokes, even very strong ones, can never be sufficient to make the wheel work. A bicycle wheel has three dozen. Not two, three, or four; not even ten would be enough. What is needed is the full complement of thirty-six. With these, rim and center are fused into one wheel.

So far I have dealt with family spirituality as if it were something apart, remote from the world. It is not, of course. The family must be connected with others. Is it possible that these human connections can become more spokes in the wheel joining edge to center?

Several years ago something happened that made it absolutely clear that the spirituality of the family could not be considered alone. Pamela and I had just moved to Maine with the two children we then had. The youngest was only a few weeks old. We had been there a short time and had learned to know only a very few people when one night about midnight we were startled by sudden, sharp cries from the baby. With the first sound I knew that these were not the normal cries of a child waking in the night. There was a quality to them that spoke of panic, of sickness, of something frightening. We rushed into the room and found the child feverish and laboring for every breath. He coughed, wheezed, and gagged. His forehead burned to the touch. It was obvious that something was seriously wrong. We called the hopsital and were told to bring him in at once.

Grimly, resolutely we bundled him with blankets, preparing him for the cold night air. I took him up in my arms and carried him downstairs as he continued his sharp, hacking cough. Outside, I paused and looked at Pamela. Should one of us go while one stayed with the older child still sleeping upstairs? Somehow that seemed impossible. We both wanted to go to the hospital. I carried the baby to the car. Pamela climbed into the front seat, took him in her arms, and waited for me to return.

I went back upstairs and into the room where our oldest child slept. There he lay, quiet, tranquil. He did not stir. I had taken his coat from the outside hallway, intending to wake him, slip his coat over his pajamas and carry him downstairs to the car to accompany us to the hospital. But he looked so peaceful there, so quiet. And all at once I wanted very much to leave him undisturbed, to let him rest just where he was, to spare him the cold night, the drive, the harsh light, the voices, the long hours of waiting for something he did not understand, a judgment on the sudden sickness of his brother. I wanted badly to spare him all this. Should I stay after all? Again I rejected the possiblity. I had to be at the hospital. Could someone else stay with him? In an instant my brain reviewed everyone I knew. Relatives were all hundreds of miles away. Old friends too were distant. I thought of those I had met recently. Many seemed good, kind people. But how would they react if I called them now, at midnight on a cold autumn night? It would not work. The problem was ours. There was no one close to help. I bent over, lifted the child from his bed, slipped on his coat as he began to wimper and complain. I lifted him into my arms and began to carry him downstairs. And at that moment I felt an emptiness such as I have never felt before. It was a sense of loneliness and of isolation that was terrible to know. We were alone.

By the next evening the child was home from the hospital, nearly recovered. Within days it was as if the incident had never happened, and yet for months afterward its memory followed me about. It remained just a step behind my consciousness each night as I checked the children before going to sleep myself. I could not forget the isolation and emptiness I had felt that night.

From that day onward I have never again thought of the family as an insular unit. It cannot be that, not if it is to survive. And yet more and more the family is being pushed in that direction. More is now being asked of the family than ever before. Husband and wife must provide all their own income, all the care for their children, do all their cooking and cleaning, and be each other's major source of companionship, affection, and support. To ask this much of a couple is really something new. In different times and different cultures it was more common for groups to work together to earn their living, for grandparents to take much of the responsibility for childcare while the parents worked, for the extended family to be close by, for there to be neighborhoods or village units, all of which expanded the center of emotional contact and support. Now this falls within the context of the family alone, and anyone who looks closely at what is now expected of husbands and wives begins to wonder less over the number of divorces than how any marriages survive at all.

Having felt the terrible sense of how isolated a family can become I am particularly interested in other models. I discovered a growing movement among some families and single people to try to counter the forces of isolation in our society with the formation of communities. For them the term *Christian community* has begun to take on a new vibrancy. Where before it often meant little more than the vague, half-hearted association of people within a parish, it has become the motto for some who are experimenting with deeper, more human connections.

I recently visited several such communities to see what they could teach me. I was not sure that I myself would feel comfortable with some of the expectations these communities placed on their members, but I suspected that in them there might at least be clues to the ways the spirituality of the family could avoid the pressure toward isolation inherent in modern life and become a vibrant part of something larger.

Of these I have selected two to reflect the diversity of what I saw: Open House Community of Lake Charles, Louisiana, and Reba Place Fellowship of Evanston, Illinois. The first is small, rural, and Catholic; the second is large, urban, and Protestant. They are different in many ways, but they both share a dedication to trying to live the fullness of the Christian message.

OPEN HOUSE COMMUNITY

Fifteen miles north of Lake Charles, along a dirt road cut into Louisiana's bayou country with its tall pines and dense underbrush, is a small cluster of buildings called Open House Community. There are a few simple structures hidden among the trees— the Community Center, four small buildings with rooms for guests, half a dozen houses, and, further back, a garage, woodworking shop, and shed for animals. A child in diapers plays on the porch of the Community Center. Beyond him older children chase each other, laughing, around a playground. A woman hangs a basket of wash upon the line, while one of the men, whose turn it is to make dinner for the group that evening, returns from the garden with a load of vegetables. Outside the garage a man repairs machinery; not far away a young man digs a small duck pond.

And in the garden men and women weed and harvest, their backs bent under the hot sun.

On the morning I arrived a large group was just returning from fishing the waters of the Gulf. They had risen before daybreak— three adults and half a dozen children—and driven forty-five miles to the coast where they unpacked their seine, a long, narrow net with floats on the top and weights below, well suited for fishing the shallow waters of the Gulf, and spent the morning dragging it through the water. Fish swim against the current, so by pulling it with the current a seining net is capable of trapping large quantities. That morning, however, something unexpected happened. They tried a new spot, a place where, because a sand bar caused water along several hundred yards of coast to eddy back on itself, the current went in a direction counter to that of the entire rest of the shore. Unfortunately, no one in their group knew that. Hour after hour they dragged their net against the current, all the time wondering why the work had become so difficult. They ended the day with only thirty fish, but also, for some reason, with about six dozen crabs.

The children who had not gone with the group crowded around as they unloaded the baskets of crabs from the car.

"What are we going to do with them all?" one woman called from the porch.

"Stew," came the answer. Other adults came to the porch, joking with those who had returned. Several of the older children unpacked the seine, carefully unrolling it and spreading it upon the grass, criss-crossing it back and forth to dry.

The three adults who had done the fishing now carried two benches outside and, with the baskets lined beside them, began cracking open the crab shells with short, strong knives, working free the tender crab meat. These three were Tom Brommelsiek, Sister Justina Baker, and Paul Thompson. Tom, a young man of twenty, has been living at the community off and on for nine months, offering his skills as general handyman. Sister Justina is a nun who, after a decade in the convent, began work with single parents in Lake Charles, joining Open House Community to learn more about families and the care of children, discovering in the process that in addition to her skill and compassion with people she truly enjoyed milking cows and fishing. Paul Thompson, a soft-spoken man with a white beard and an easy smile, had been at Open House with his wife, Selma, and their five children longer than anyone else. It was his vision that had first brought the community together. These three bent over the shellfish, children hopping excitedly around them, and joked with each other about how long it had taken them to realize that they were pulling the net against the current.

"Did you see any big fish?" one small boy asked.

"I saw a shark," said Tom.

The boy's eyes grew large.

"It was only a sand shark, though. Sand sharks are only about so long," Tom said, laying down his knife and stretching out his hands a foot and a half or so. "They can't hurt you."

"That didn't stop you from jumping about two feet into the air when you saw it," Sister Justina said, laughing.

"It brushed right against my leg," Tom said, picking up his knife and beginning to work on the crab again. "How was I to know it was only a little sand shark?"

As the crabs were cleaned, they were carried into the kitchen. Already the water for stew was boiling on the stove.

Open House Community began in 1971, but its story starts ten years earlier when Paul Thompson was twenty-six years old. He and Selma had been married three years and the two of them were struggling to get Paul's young architectural business established when an offer came for a partnership that would open up the possibility of state contracts. Against Selma's better judgment, Paul took the offer.

His business prospered. Only slowly did he see that he was being drawn into a world with its own rules, its own rewards, a world of corruption. Later he wrote:

I first learned about competition in the marketplace. Beating the other fellow to the most lucrative job was *always* right, regardless of the method used. Manipulation, misrepresentation, outright lies and payoffs were all okay, because the little motto "business is business" covered it all. After we had elbowed our way into the favorite position with state politicians, we were able to buy a good commission for a public building. The way the system worked was simple. Before an architect was awarded a state contract, he had to kick back 10 percent of his commission in cash. That was simply "the cost of doing business." I paid that cash to the policeman who was sent to our office to pick it up. Three days later we would receive a contract in the mail signed by the Governor. Simple, quick, easy . . .[1]

It was a year and a half before Paul Thompson could admit to himself the true depth of the corruption in which he was involved. Then suddenly he wanted out, but by that time he was deeply implicated, and it was also well known that fatal "accidents" could be arranged for anyone who suddenly stopped cooperating with the system. Paul found himself horribly entangled in a net of terrifying and dangerous connections. Any struggle threatened only to wrap it all the more tightly around him.

And yet some of what he had learned in the past few months turned out to be useful knowledge. He had learned the inner workings of the system well enough to know in what ways he was most tightly bound to it. Slowly, carefully, he began to cut those ties. With the help of lawyers and bankers he began to separate himself little by little. He could not move too quickly or he would call attention to himself. It took him over a year to cut himself free. In the process he voluntarily surrendered all of his newly acquired wealth.

Paul hoped at first that giving up all the money he had gained would ease his conscience, but a sense of guilt haunted him. Finally he could stand it no longer. Terrified at his own resolve, he appeared before state officials and gave an account of the state's system of professional-political kickbacks to the extent of his knowledge and involvement. The facts were given. Everything was recorded in the transcript of the hearing. But the day after the hearing the transcript disappeared. Reporters, investigating committees, and judges tried for months to get hold of it. All were told that it had been misplaced.

Finally Paul was subpoenaed to appear before a grand jury. He sat in the courtroom waiting to be called to testify again. Instead, the district attorney took the floor. In his hand he held the "misplaced" transcript. Standing before the grand jury holding the transcript, the district attorney asked if they could see any evidence that would warrant further investigation. The foreman rose and announced that they saw none. The transcript was never shown; Paul was never given a chance to testify. The case was closed.

Paul had lost his business, most of his money, and made some powerful enemies. Painfully and methodically he and Selma began all over again and tried to re-establish his architectural business, now on a smaller scale. But their recent experiences continued as a preoccupation and they became actively involved in efforts to reform local politics.

Soon Paul's architectural business again began to prosper and he and Selma were respected members of the community with a large house in the suburbs and a membership at the country club, but Paul began to see that all of this was possible only because of more subtle forms of corruption and crimes against others. At the age of thirty-five, with five children to support, Paul decided to go to law school. He and Selma sold their house to pay for the tuition.

Then with law school only a few days away, the Thompsons and several other families went together on a Labor Day picnic. From the start there was something special about the day. The food was shared, children played together, adults talked—a pleasant outing in every way, but there was something else as well; an unexpectedly strong feeling of love and acceptance pervaded.

Stretched out on the grass, talking to several others, Paul fell asleep, awakening an hour later to find that the others, still talking, had left him undisturbed. And resting there amidst the warmth of the day and the warmth of the people around him, Paul Thompson all at once had a vision, a glimpse at an entirely different way of life than he had ever known before, one of families sharing their property, their money, their lives—owning all things together and giving all their effort to each other.

The vision would not let him go. Hours later it still gripped his imagination. Finally late that evening he sat down and began to try to work it out on paper. The more he studied it, the more possible it seemed. Overwhelmed with excitement he described to Selma what he had in mind. Her enthusiasm was immediate. That very night she called five other couples and invited them to join them the following evening to discuss the plan.

At first they all seemed interested, but the more it was discussed and the closer it came to reality, the more reluctant most became. In the end only two families stuck with it—the Thompsons and one other. They took all they had, formed it into a common fund, and bought sixty acres. They moved onto the land in 1971 and began building a few simple homes around a community center.

Those early years were a time of exploration. The Gospels were their inspiration, but they made no effort to make the Christian origin of the community a visible part of their way of life. And yet many outside of the community began to find something special there. Open House Community took its name very seriously. Everyone was welcome, those who were curious and wanted to learn, those who were homeless and wanted shelter, those who had suffered and needed care—all who asked were taken in. Many, many asked. There were so many that for Paul most have blurred into a memory of indistinguishable faces arriving one after another. He writes that

faces of the many hurt and crushed victims of our unworkable society come to me as I think back—people who came to us in need—alcoholics, beaten and pregnant women, runaways, educated men with defeated spirits, and children who cried for home, stability and a little love. . . . We did what little we could which was never enough. . . .[2]

They came and went. And during this time members of the community also came and went. There was then no agreement even of what it meant to be a part of the community. Several families arrived only to stay for a few months, several others remained for years. Only the Thompsons—Paul and Selma and the children—remained throughout, joined in 1974 by the McNallys —Ed and Flo and their small son, James.

Photographs of this period show playfulness and joy, children watching rabbits in their pen, children and adults laughing, romping, deeply engrossed in games. The photographs show a very real side of their life, but there was another as well. More and more a sense of confusion and conflicting expectations was felt. The vision was there; it had been there from the start, but it had not been brought into focus. "In those days," Paul said, "we thought that all we had to do was live together and share our possessions for there to be a community. We were wrong. We needed something more."

Some left, others joined. By the spring of 1976, five years after the first members had moved to Open House Community, only the Thompsons and McNallys had been with the group any length of time. Everyone else had come within the last two or three months.

It was at that time that Don and Jackie Williams came to visit. They lead Agape, a small community in the mountains of Tennessee. The Williams had come to discuss ways in which the two communities might share with one another. Their visit was to change everything.

The entire community was sitting in the common room. Don Williams kept pressing them to describe their reason for being together and the source of their strength. "What is your center?" he kept pressing them. For a long time no one was quite sure what he was asking. Only slowly did they begin to see that what he wanted them to show him was the very thing that they had been missing all along. "Make Christ your center," he said. And with these words it was as if a chasm had opened down the middle of the room, because to four people, Ed and Flo McNally and Paul and Selma Thompson, it was instantly obvious that this was what they wanted, and they each knew with equal clearness that the other three felt the same. The others in the room also saw that the community was about to change, but they knew that the change was not for them. From that moment forward Open House was transformed. All saw it. Some wanted to be a part of that transformation, others did not.

Open House seemed on the edge of a new beginning and yet within two months of the Williamses' visit the place was nearly empty. Most left because they did not like the new direction the community had taken. In August 1976, the Thompsons left too, but in their case it was because they wanted even more than Open House then seemed able to offer. Paul had decided that to participate in a truly Christ-centered community they should move to Agape in Tennessee. Selma disagreed, feeling that their task was where they were, but decided to trust Paul's intuition.

The first chills of autumn found only the McNallys at Open House Community. Ed and Flo now had a second child, and Ed's mother, Dorothy, had recently retired and taken one of the community's houses so that there were five in all. It had been written into the community's original agreement that if the group should disband, the property and buildings would be donated to a court-awarded charity. Although it looked as if the community was now dead, the McNallys had decided they would stay on until it became clear what should be done with the property. There was some hope of turning it into a retreat center.

For them that winter was a time of listening, waiting, and loneliness, a time haunted by the emptiness of the homes that had been filled with friends and the darkness of the Community Center which had to be closed down and locked to save costs. That winter was one of the coldest in recent years. With no one inside to keep the rooms heated many of the pipes burst. So close to what had at first appeared a renewal of the community, it had suddenly died.

It was a long, harsh winter for the McNallys, struggling with their feelings of abandonment and depression, and for the Thompsons in Tennessee, and yet almost imperceptibly, new roots were reaching out. Ed McNally was the first to find his own springtime. He writes:

[I had reached] a point where I couldn't see God in anything. I have for many years suffered from both anxiety and depression to varying degrees, but the most recent depression was the deepest and most painful. Not only was I deep in misery with myself and others, but at the same time becoming aware that the Lord was weaning me from the security of self—a self not even happy with itself. . . . I read somewhere that you spend a lot of time developing your ego only to give it over to the Lord from whom you came. [One night when the depression was at its worst] Fr. Sam Jacobs came out and spent quite some time praying over me for baptism in the spirit, release of the gifts, and inner healing. I did not lose control as I feared; I was reserved yet submitting, anxious yet at peace. . . . Since that night I have experienced an even deeper love of the Lord and of myself and those around me.[3]

The entire family was beginning to find what it meant to be centered in the Lord. No longer did they feel abandoned. Instead, they felt God's love for them and their own love for each other. They felt peace. Ed McNally describes one evening:

Late Saturday, the weekend of Thanksgiving, I was alone in the garden transplanting beets and kohlrabi when suddenly the wind began to blow through the tall pines and move across my face, and I felt God's presence strongly in the wind. I began to chant the words used often in prayer at Agape Community—"Holy is God . . . Holy the Mighty One . . . Holy the Immortal One. . . ." I felt a deep oneness with our loved ones there and was at once participating in their evening prayer. The wind blew again, and I knew the joy coming from the Charismatic conference in Lafayette—the song, the healing, the prophecy. The two winds had crossed. I heard the Lord call my name, and I also heard Flo calling me for supper.[4]

Then, one by one, people began to return. In February the Thompsons also returned. Their six months in Tennessee had taught them that their place was at Open House Community.

Out of a long cold winter in which the community had all but withered and died, it grew again, reborn, stronger now, more vibrant. Much that was superficial and extraneous had fallen away. It was in some ways starker now and simpler, but also more supple and firmly rooted in the conviction that God was their center. All had learned much about themselves and about the strengths and the limits of community. They hoped to proceed cautiously and not to hurry the tender new growth, and yet their enthusiasm and excitement could hardly be held back. Something extraordinary was occurring. Paul wrote at the time:

It was just a gentle call which brought a small group of people together from scattered points of the compass—Louisiana, Tennessee, Ohio, Arkansas and Minnesota. The most important thing we all held in common was a deep desire to abandon our lives to the direction provided by God. For all of us it was at least our third attempt at community life, and we knew the hardships involved in close personal relationships.

So we gathered together in early February open to whatever happened with us, but determined to submit all decisions to God in prayer. And that's what brought about so many positive changes. We are a far more peaceful people now, more active, better organized, have greater degrees of personal responsibility and are growing in mature faith. Maybe the most dramatic change in the last few months has been the way we make decisions. We now understand consensus as a state of mind and spirit which exists before we come together to make decisions. And so we are learning to think and act as one unified whole. We no longer try to force decision making into a specific time span, but just let the Lord work in our hearts over a period of days, or even weeks. Always someone is inspired with a key thought which gains instantaneous acceptance of the entire group.

We are growing in enthusiasm about community life, and are in constant awe about the way our prayers are answered. As Laura Thompson was telling Ed's mom last week, "You know, Dorothy, there *are* miracles happening at Open House Community!"[5]

One of the first changes, then, was the method of decision making. All matters were brought to the group, not so much so that everyone could give his or her opinion, as that each member could help discern God's will for them. Decision making had become an act of prayer.

And prayer itself was now a part of community life. A small chapel was built in the Community Center and three times each day the group gathered there for a short period of prayer. A longer prayer meeting was held every Wednesday evening, one with song, teaching, and sharing, and one that quickly began to draw people from outside the group. A priest who had earlier spent several months at the Open House Community received permission from his bishop to temporarily make the community his home. He joined them in the spring of 1977. The Eucharist was now also part of the regular life of the community.

But the greatest change was in the group's own understanding of community. "We thought in the beginning," Paul said, "that community was simply a lifestyle, a set of external conditions. We assumed that if a group of us got together, lived near one another, and shared what we owned, we would have a community. We found that that was not true. Community is what the Lord gives to people who are willing to give up everything. It is not the product of one way of life or another."

By making God their center and their source, so much that had before seemed important began to seem much less important. On the other hand they came to value all the more what they offered each other. They marveled at the gentle bonds with which God had tied their lives together, and they recognized their relationships to each other for the first time for what they truly were—not just friendships or passing alliances of like-minded people, but something deeper, far deeper, and more lasting. They had joined their economic, personal, and spiritual destinies into one close association, joined for richer or for poorer, for better or for worse, each accepting the needs of the others as a responsibility equal to his or her own.

Almost as soon as the community was reunited, it began work on a written covenant intended to formalize the tie that joined them together. It would be a vow, one taken for life, a vow not intended to create what was not there, but, like the vow of marriage, to acknowledge the bond that had already formed, and so to deepen and strengthen it. It took several months and many drafts before the two paragraphs of that covenant were at last complete. The first paragraph is a statement of what the community is and intended to be, the second a statement of each member's actual commitment. It reads:

We are a Covenant Community in the Roman Catholic tradition, subject to the authority of our Bishop and to our designated leadership. Our life is centered in God: the Father, the Son, and the Holy Spirit, our model of perfect community. We understand ourselves to be in God's image more fully as a community rather than as individual persons; and together we aspire to a life of Gospel poverty.

I enter into this Covenant as an act of faith, of hope, and of love in our Lord Jesus Christ from whom all of my strength comes. I commit and dedicate myself, all that I have and all that I am, without reservation, to the Lord Jesus Christ and to my brothers and sisters in Community. I understand this commitment as an act of total abandonment of my whole self to the will of God. I desire and agree to submit all my personal decisions to the community for its discernment.

By the summer of 1977 the covenant had taken its final form, but once written it seemed too much. As Selma Thompson recalls: "At last we finished writing. We had finally managed to say all that community meant to us. But now that it was done we read it over, looked at one another and said, 'I can't sign that. I can't live that way, no one can.' Then we went back and tried to cut it, and make it easier to live with. We cut one part, but put it back, then another part but put it back too. We checked and rechecked every phrase. In the end it stayed just as we had written it. The statement said just what we wanted it to say. It was now up to us to decide whether that was really the life we wanted to live."

It took them over two years to decide. It was on October 20, 1979, that four people, two couples—Paul and Selma Thompson and Ed and Flo McNally—formally signed the covenant in each other's presence during an outdoor Mass held at the Open House Community.

Although there can be as many as forty people living at Open House Communtiy, these two couples remain the only Covenant Members. Another couple is undergoing the long period of discernment that precedes this membership. Others making up the community are children, who cannot become members until they become adults, and those staying with the community on a temporary basis. "Temporary" may mean months or even years.

At Open House, the day begins at seven A.M. when the community gathers in the chapel for a Eucharistic service, then goes to share breakfast in the Community Center. Work begins at eight-thirty. Most people work at the community. Some garden, some care for the animals, some paint and build, or repair the cars and machinery. Others wash or cook, or, in season, put up the vegetables they have grown. Paul Thompson conducts his architectural business from an office in the Community Center. Only two or three leave for jobs with outside businesses.

At noon the community again gathers in the chapel for prayer and reciting of psalms. Lunch is at twelve-thirty. The hour from one to two P.M. is for rest and quiet. The younger children spend that time at home or else playing quietly. At two o'clock those who have a specific job to complete, or who want to return to work, do. Others use the time from two to five to study or to follow their own pursuits.

At five o'clock all gather in the Common Room to coordinate plans for the following day. After this they again gather in the chapel for prayer, then in the dining room for supper.

On Wednesday evening there is a prayer meeting, on Saturday evening, Mass. Both of these draw many people from beyond the community. All other evenings of the week are free.

It is a way of life that blends the life of the center with that of the desert to a remarkable degree. Soon after joining the group Flo McNally listed three ways in which living in community helped her as a mother:

1. There is so much sharing of the workload [that] I have more time to spend with my baby. And when I *am* busy—or tired—or sick—I know there will be a loving, dependable adult or young person to care for James even if daddy isn't available.
2. Here I can observe good mothering and get helpful advice and encouragement from more experienced mothers.
3. There is plenty of adult companionship available at the community, so I don't feel the isolation from other adults many young mothers and fathers feel after they first become parents.

Community living offers James many advantages also. He gets to spend a lot of time with *both* his parents. He has lots of other children to play with and learn from. He is certainly thriving on all the love he's getting here, and in his 15-month-old way, he reflects this love to others.[6]

All work is shared. Men, women, and older children all take part in the cooking. Each meal is prepared entirely by one person, although those just learning to cook and mothers with nursing children are given help.

"It's really not at all hard to cook for that many people," Selma Thompson told me. "You easily adjust. And with everyone taking a turn it gives us all so much more time for other things. Before we moved into the community I would no sooner finish preparing one meal than I started the next. Now I cook several meals a week and have so much more time for other things. I love to cook, but I love it so much more now that I am doing it less."

The work of maintaining the community is also divided. Painting, carpentry, washing, auto repair, work in the community's large garden, care of the animals—there are a wide variety of things to do and each is done according to people's ability and interest. The community is close to being self-sufficient, but what expenses they have are met by what Paul Thompson earns through architectural work and what the one or two others who have outside jobs contribute.

I asked Paul if he saw it as a weakness of the group that so many are dependent on the support of so few.

"Not at all," he said. "Everyone here works. Some of our work brings in an income, some of our work does not, but all of it is necessary. Without our large gardens, our cows and chickens, without doing our own car repairs, our own canning, without our carefully planned cooking, without doing all our own building, painting, and repairs, the money that is brought in would be meaningless. The little money that comes is able to meet our needs only because, through everyone's effort, our needs are so few. Every job here is essential."

Shared work, shared childcare, ministry to those who come seeking help, shared daily worship—in many ways Open House

Community has joined the life at the edge with that at the center. For those who seek solitude and complete withdrawal, there is even a small cabin back in the woods with a cot, desk, and chair. Everyone there has more time and opportunity for prayer, for helping others, for self-development—for that combination of self-growth and care for others that can be so difficult to bring together within the context of the family alone.

I noticed two problems, however. The first is that the family really is not the center I believe it should be. Individuals are important and the community is important. The family, although emphasized, is not as distinctive as it might be. This was apparent in many different ways. Several people admitted to me, for example, that they wished there were more opportunity for family meals not shared with others in the community. And the meals the group shared in the Common Room did have a certain impersonalness—like meals in a cafeteria. There was neither intimacy nor a sense of special community connection.

A second weakness was that this is both a community—that is, a group working to establish close and lasting ties among its members—and a center for hospitality, taking in people for shorter or longer times. Many of those who come to stay have little interest in community as such. This coming and going gives a transience to the group. Members of the community expend large amounts of energy on those who will stay for relatively short periods, leaving little energy for each other. Many felt burned out and exhausted and, when I visited, this problem had reached crisis proportion. There was talk of Open House Community redefining itself.*

I sat in on a prayer meeting when the problem was brought before the community.

"We need all your prayers and thoughts," Flo McNally told the group. "Meditate on this in the coming weeks. Is the Lord asking something new of Open House Community, or is this emptiness that many of us feel just part of a rededication?"

Very little was said in response. Most seemed content to follow

---

* Open House Community recently changed its name to Holy City Community.

Flo's suggestion, to simply wait and let the answer slowly stir from within their thoughts and prayers.

One woman, however, spoke out. She had been shifting impatiently in her seat as Flo spoke, and now she was angry. "I came here to pray and sing," she said, "not discuss community business."

"It's all a part of our life together," Flo said. "I brought it up so that we could pray about it as a group."

The woman said nothing more but during the next song she left.

The following day while painting ceilings with Tom Brommelsiek, the young man who had been seining in the Gulf on the day I arrived, I asked him what it was like to live so close with so many people.

He pushed his roller back and forth in the tray of paint and surveyed the bit of ceiling we had yet to do.

"It's hard," he said. "Sometimes I think it's about the hardest thing there is." He raised his roller and went back and forth in long, even strokes. He paused for a moment to wipe up a drop of paint that had missed the drop cloth.

"It's hard," he said again, "but nothing teaches you more about yourself. You see yourself much more clearly than you might want."

We worked several minutes in silence. Tom paused once to refill both trays with paint.

"Do you plan to stay in the community?" I asked.

"I'm considering it," he said. "I like work. I like carpentry, auto repair, and even"—he waved his roller in a small flourish—"painting, but I keep thinking that it is also necessary to somehow make your living loving people. Here a person does just that. Of course its not a 'living' the way most Americans think of it. Here living means simply to live and also to love. It's a special place."

He put down his roller and studied the finished ceiling.

"That looks pretty good," he said. "Let's see if we can do as well on the next room."*

---

* Open House Community

REBA PLACE FELLOWSHIP

I arrived at the Reba Place Fellowship late in the afternoon of the third of July. The day had been a hot one, humid, close and still—unbroken by any breeze. A thin haze still hung among the trees, but evening was approaching and already the air was growing cooler.

Reba Place is in Evanston, Illinois, a suburb of Chicago. A university town, some of Evanston has large, elegant homes, well-kept shops, fountains, and parks lining the shores of Lake Michigan; the impression is of a wealthy, comfortable, secure place. But the neighborhood where Reba Place is located is a little different. The yards are small; the homes—some badly in need of repair—are set among low-rise apartment buildings. The population is largely black and Hispanic. Driving past the large homes of Evanston, a person might pass block after block without ever seeing another human being. Around Reba Place life is everywhere. Within the space of two or three houses I saw an old man who had stopped to chat with another rocking back and forth on a porch swing, a group of teenagers lounging against one of the cars parked along the street, and a line of children chasing each other and laughing as they darted in front of me to disappear behind one of the houses. Farther on, two women who had been talking together stopped to call to a third who crossed the street to join them.

As I walked I checked the number of each house. Before one I stopped, then pulled a paper from my pocket to confirm the address. A young woman sitting on the steps looked up from the book she was reading. I told her that I had come to visit Reba Place Fellowship. She smiled and invited me inside, saying that the woman in charge of guests would be with me in several minutes.

Reba Place's roots are Anabaptist, a name taken during the Reformation from Greek words meaning re-baptizers, since their belief in adult baptism was originally misunderstood as a call to two baptisms. In nearly all areas Anabaptist thought agreed with that of other Protestants—accepting the Apostles Creed, the triune

God, the incarnation and atoning work of Christ, and the authority of the Scriptures—yet the Anabaptists are often described as
part of the radical Reformation because of their tendency to push
every teaching just as far as it could go. And there was in fact a
radical character to the very nature of the movement. The Anabaptists had no one theology. They consistently resisted any move
that would have brought the teachings of any of their leaders to
the forefront. The emphasis was on individual interpretation. The
Anabaptists were very much a popular movement. All were considered equally qualified to hear and to preach the Word. Leaders
and preachers did emerge, because their gifts were recognized, but
their words were to be accepted only after individual examination.
It was a movement of the disenfranchized and the powerless, and
where the other Protestant groups and the Catholics quickly found
their positions merged with political issues—with theology all too
often held up by kings and powerful lords as a mask to cover their
struggle for territories and influence—the Anabaptists actively
disassociated themselves from any temporal ambitions, either local, national, or international. Pacifists, who considered the Lord
alone their master, they had from the beginning a strong inclination toward communal living and so early on earned the distrust
and hatred of everyone else.

It was under the weight of persecution that the tendency toward
communal life grew stronger. In the 1530s some of the Moravian
Anabaptists banded together and pooled their possessions. The
early days of this brotherhood—*Bruderhof* as it was called—were
hard ones. There was dissension and harsh disagreement within
the group. Only under the leadership of a man named Jacob Hutter was the group able to rally together. One observer described
them this way:

Christian community of goods was practiced according to the teaching of
Christ. . . . All shared alike . . . there being, of course, special provisions
for the sick and for the children. . . .

Swords were forged into pruning hooks, saws, and other useful imple-
ments. . . . Every one was his fellow man's brother and all lived together

in harmony. . . . Revenge was forever done away. Patience was their only weapon in all difficulties.

They were subject to the authorities and obedient in all good works, in all things that are not contrary to God, the faith, and conscience. What was due the government in the form of taxes or customs was paid . . . , since the government is ordained by God and is an institution as necessary in this evil world as the daily bread. . . .

No cursing nor swearing was heard. . . . There was no betting, no dancing and card-playing, no carousing nor drinking. They did not make for themselves fashion, immodest, proud and unsuitable clothes. . . . There was no singing of shameful songs . . . but Christian and spiritual songs, and the songs of Bible stories.[7]

Jacob Hutter was arrested and killed in 1536, but the group came to call themselves Hutterites. Nearly all Hutterites were slaughtered in the early weeks of the Thirty Years War, and yet even today in the United States, Canada, and England there are Hutterite and Bruderhof communities that draw directly from that original inspiration.[8] Most of the Anabaptists who came to America, however, were Mennonites, who took their name from Menno Simon, one of the early leaders of the Dutch Anabaptists. Reba Place's connection with the Anabaptists is through this Mennonite heritage.

The woman in charge of guests arrived and introduced herself. I was told that the Lukens family would be responsible for my stay at Reba Place. David Lukens arrived several minutes later. A thin, gentle man, he is a college teacher most of the year but was working that summer with the community's construction crew. On our way to the guest house David gave me a tour of the neighborhood.

The day was now much cooler. A breeze had dispelled the haze and the sky remained bright with the lingering sunlight of the late summer evening. Many people were out, some sitting on porches, others strolling along the sidewalk, couples, friends, children.

"Reba Place gets its name," David said, "from the street where the five people who began the community first lived. As the group grew, it expanded to other streets, but always within an area of four or five blocks. No house in the community is more than a ten-minute walk from any other."

David waved to many of those we passed, and several times he stopped to talk. Continuing on, he pointed out the homes of the members. All we went by at first were older houses, well cared for and of a size intended for one family, but at the corner we paused before one much larger, built in an imitation Gothic style popular just before the turn of the century.

"This is also one of the community's houses," David said. "We are in the process of dividing it into apartments. It needs work inside and out—a coat of paint, a new roof. The community has its own construction company, the Just Builders, which employs eight men year-round and others, like myself, when the work gets heavy. The Just Builders remain pretty busy just doing the work that has to be done in the community, but they do work for others too. It is high-quality work at a low price so word has gotten around, and they have more requests for jobs than they can possibly handle. They have to turn most away."

Turning left on a cross street, we walked down another block until again David stopped, this time before a four-story brick apartment complex.

"This is owned by the community also. We have several apartment buildings, each with about twenty units ranging in size from one to three bedrooms. After buying the building we go through it from roof to basement, cleaning, making structural improvements and redoing all apartments—replastering, rewiring, sanding and staining the wood, and painting. The finished apartments are lovely. We try to limit the number of community members who live in these buildings to about one third of the total number of residents. There is a terrible need in this neighborhood for quality housing at an affordable price. We hope to provide that with these buildings. Also, opening these apartments to those beyond the community has become a ministry in itself. There is a great deal of help and sharing that goes on between community members and their neighbors in these buildings."

At Reba Place no one has an independent income. All salaries—and for full members, all assets—are turned over to the community. Each family is given an allowance adequate to meets its needs. The allowance may be higher or lower than the paycheck that had been contributed because it is based entirely on each family's requirements. Pooling resources in this way allows each member to follow his or her call. It becomes possible for some to work full-time for the community or for a volunteer service group and know that their needs will be met. At Reba Place it is the Lord's work that is important, not money. People live comfortably, but without luxury. And many things, such as cars, are shared.

I asked one woman what it felt like to move from being a family providing for itself to one supported by and supporting the group.

"The strongest feeling," she said, "was one of intense relief. Before we moved here we had a good income. It took every bit of our time and energy to get it, but as long as we were careful we could buy what we needed. And yet we were so alone, and because of that, so vulnerable. Sickness, fire, a lost job—what if suddenly we needed help? Insurance is no answer. In times of hardship people need other people as well as money. God made us to depend on one another, and it is a sad person who goes through life pretending he can get by alone. Coming here, we gave up some of what we had, but I could not even tell you anymore what that was. We have everything we need. It is a wonderful feeling."

Including children and those considering membership there are over two hundred and fifty people at Reba Place Fellowship. Most of these are families who take into their homes one or two additional fellowship members to share all their activities, meals, and responsibilities—who become, in fact, part of the family. Some families, usually those whose children have grown, become the core of larger groups—households they are called—where a variety of different people, usually singles, but also perhaps a young married couple or a single parent, come together under one roof to form from their separateness something unified and strong.

Households, extended families, nuclear families, singles—in the end these differences in living arrangements matter little because there are many ways in which everyone is drawn into the activities of the community. Everyone, for example, is a member of a Small Group. Small Groups consist of anywhere from eight to twenty people. They meet at least twice a week, once for prayer and discussion and once for fun. Small Groups gather for outings, for birthdays, for holidays, or for no particular reason at all. They also become the core for support if one of their members need help. Tightly bound together, these Small Groups are an important component of community life.

No one selects his or her own Small Group. New members are assigned by Elders who make every effort to fit each person or couple to the group, while working to give each group as much diversity as possible, balancing married with singles, older with younger, those with children with those without. Each group has a leader, or, more often, leaders, since the most common pattern is for a husband and wife to share the responsibility. In addition to general companionship and support, the Small Groups have another task as well—they actively work to promote the health and spiritual growth of their members.

"It often happens," one woman explained, "that in the process of praying and sharing together, some of the pain, fear, or anger that people have hidden from themselves begins to work its way out, and one of the main functions of the Small Group is to help to heal that pain, that fear, or that anger. And you would be surprised at how genuine the healing can be.

"It can also happen that a person will find through the group that he or she has a special gift, a God-given talent he or she may hardly have suspected. It is then the job of the Small Group to support and encourage that as well."

Each Small Group is connected to one of three associations of Small Groups called "clusters." Reba Place Fellowship has grown so rapidly—its numbers quadrupled in the last eight years—that the Elders began to worry that it was becoming too large for anyone to find an easy identification with the full group. Clusters of Small Groups were formed to provide a wider contact with the community on a manageable scale. Each cluster gathers about once a month for a meal or an outing.

The community as a whole gathers every Friday evening for a common dinner, then again on Sunday for worship.

Family or household, Small Group, cluster, community—these are the units, the ever widening circles of associations, that form Reba Place Fellowship into a cohesive whole. In practice the structure is quite simple, each division established to meet a specific need. And yet, simple as it is, it is the product of a long evolution from far simpler beginnings.

The story of Reba Place begins in the spring of 1953, in Europe, at a conference attended by seven young American Mennonite graduate students. The conference ended but the students lingered for several days sharing ideas and the hopes and doubts they had for their church. There was an energy and enthusiasm working in all of them, but there was something else as well, an uneasiness about what seemed to them two conflicting movements within the church. On the one hand there was a rediscovery of the Anabaptist roots of the Mennonites. Historians such as John Horsh and Harold S. Bender were helping the church uncover the origins of their movement, pointing out for them the value of that first vision of a powerfully committed membership lead by the laity, dedicated to peace and equality, and with a strong communal concern. On the other hand the church itself seemed to be moving in another direction altogether, toward a professionally trained clergy presiding over services that were more social than spiritual gatherings of a membership that had come largely to accept the values of the society around them. As they talked, these seven young men became more and more convinced that it was to the vision of the early Anabaptists that they must remain true, that it was there that God's spirit was expressed, there that God's power could be felt, there that they would find a renewal for the church.

Their time together ended and they went their separate ways. Four remained in Europe to continue their study. Three returned to the United States. Among those who returned was John Miller, who had taken a teaching position at Goshen College, a Mennonite school in Indiana. There he continued the discussions begun in Europe with some of his students. Several began to meet for worship services in his home.

Meanwhile, the discussions in Europe had taken a concrete form. The group of seven had arranged to bring their ideas together in a series of pamphlets. The first issue of *Concern: A Pamphlet Series* appeared in June of 1954 and contained, in addition to an unsigned introduction, two articles, "Toward an Understanding of the Decline of the West" by Paul Peachey and "The Anabaptist Dissent: the Logic of the Place of the Disciple in Society" by John Howard Yoder; both authors were among the seven who had met in Europe. They and the other five were all listed as publishers.

Concern was, as an editorial note states,

an independent pamphlet series dealing with current Mennonite and general Christian issues. Its character is semi-popular and is designed to stimulate informal discussion and common searching within the brotherhood for a strengthening of prophetic Christian faith and conduct.[9]

Stimulate discussion it did. Within the group of American Mennonites it reached it was explosive, a radical call to a reassessment of a way of life that had come to find an all too comfortable place in American society. The essays covered a wide range of subjects and yet, despite the variety of topics, the center of attention seldom wandered far from the effort to turn the contemporary church back to its original Anabaptist revelation.

The second issue of *Concern* dealt with the contemporary church exclusively. John Howard Yoder and David Shank wrote "Biblicism and the Church," Paul Peachey "Spirit and Form in the Church of Christ." John Miller had an article called "The Church in the Old Testament," which, despite its title, was really about the failings of the institution of today's Christianity. He writes:

Perhaps the most obvious failure in the contemporary church . . . is the absence of any real "hungering and thirsting" for the manifestation of God's reign in the near future. . . . More . . . is needed to overcome the extremely "this world" orientation of western Christendom. . . .

[The church has come to identify] herself with the cultural and political forces that surround her, thus accepting both the world's attitude and approach to the enemy. For the church in the United States, for example, there is no more disturbing fact than the widespread acceptance by "Christian" people of the militaristic institutions as both necessary and right. . . .

The multiplication of large, unwieldy congregations, the ever resurgent cult of the popular preacher, the almost universally accepted practice of concentrating in the hands of the few the responsibility for exercising spiritual gifts have often tended to make the Sunday morning gatherings at the church pious theatricals, where nothing more is expected than a little entertainment, a little peace of mind, and perhaps a little challenge to nobler living. There are all too few Sunday morning gatherings at the church about which an outsider would spontaneously exclaim: "God is really among you" (1 Cor. 14:25). It is perhaps this defect at the core of her worship experience that more than anything else vitiates the testimony and effectiveness of the church in today's world.[10]

To many young people in college or serving with Mennonite service groups the assessments in *Concern* seemed all too accurate, and the small series of pamphlets became something of a rallying cry. People began speaking of the "*Concern* Movement." It had an excitement and a freshness and offered what seemed a clearer, truer way into the future.

Others, however, saw *Concern* differently. To some of the church leaders the issues raised by *Concern* seemed at best unrealistic and at worst disruptive and radical.

The controversy was particularly apparent at Goshen College. A number of the students there enthusiastically embraced and even broadened the ideas set forth in *Concern*, only to feel increasingly strong opposition from Harold S. Bender, the very man whose pioneering historical work on the early Anabaptists had originally inspired the group, and who was now dean of the college. For two years, 1955 and 1956, there was a smouldering atmosphere of dissent and disagreement at Goshen. In classrooms and in dorm rooms discussion and argument raged. The issues presented in *Concern* would just not die but continued and grew. And yet at no time did the disagreements burst forth to take a public form. Although everyone was aware of what was happening, it remained a struggle kept tightly under the surface.

Only concerning John Miller did official disapproval make itself felt. After John returned from Europe, students and some of the younger faculty began to gather in his home to worship together. The group grew steadily. They had soon grown so large that they had to rent a building from Goshen to hold their services. In time they began to celebrate on their own the Lord's Supper. For them it was a return to the lay ministry of their Anabaptist roots, but to the leadership at Goshen it seemed a highly controversial and disruptive move coming at the very time when the church was trying to establish clearly visible pastoral leadership. The group was banned from using the building and sternly warned against continued meetings of this sort.

Stung by the harshness of the reprimand, most of the group retreated, but a few continued, once more meeting in John Miller's home. This time they gathered simply to pray together and talk, avoiding any of the activities that might be seen as a challenge to the regular worship service. But slowly within this small group a pattern of care and support began to emerge. Almost before they knew what was happening, they found themselves intimately involved in each other's spiritual and material well-being. Not the result of planning or discussion, the seeds of community seemed to be taking root entirely on their own, growing naturally from their shared prayer and from the depth of the interest in one another that resulted.

In the third issue of *Concern* John Miller and Norman Kraus tried to generalize about what they were seeing develop in that small prayer group:

If, however, we dare point this [*Concern*] movement to the direction in which we believe the spirit is leading us, it is to what might be called "the passion for community." . . . The Spirit works "togetherness." The Spirit creates *koinonia,* a quality of togetherness that is undoubtedly far more real than most contemporary Christians can even imagine, for it is the togetherness of the *habhura* (Aramaic for *koinonia*), which in the New Testament times undoubtably meant a fellowship powerful enough to include within itself a kind of communism of goods. Such at least was the *habhura* of Jesus with his disciples.

The primary thing then is that the Spirit awaken us to the sin of our self-sufficient, independent ways, and stir up within us the love for community.[11]

The group at Goshen continued to gain an ever deeper understanding of what community meant. They even began to share their goods among themselves.

Then in the spring of 1957 John Miller was notified that his job at Goshen would not be available to him the following year. No reason was given, but his views and his involvement with *Concern* had been a constant irritation. By then, however, the road seemed clear. John and his wife and several who had been with them were determined to continue their experiment in community. They bought a house in Evanston, Illinois. Near Chicago where they felt so much of their work would probably be, and yet not urban itself, Evanston seemed an ideal place to establish a community. There were five in that earliest group, John Miller and his wife, John and Joanna Lehman who had been students at Goshen, and one other young man, also a former Goshen student. Their address in Evanston was 727 Reba Place.

Since then there have been many changes. Transformation has been part of the character of Reba Place and yet in retrospect there seem six distinct stages to its history.

In its earliest stage Reba Place remained much as it began. In the years that followed the move to Evanston a few more families joined, and others who did not live there came to think of Reba Place as their spiritual home, but the group remained small. For a short time all members of the community lived in one house, then, when that became too cramped, in a building with several different apartments. When two or three of the families began to have children and outgrow the apartments, a few houses were bought within a block or so of each other.

All buildings were purchased by the group as a whole. From the beginning all salaries and assets went into a common fund to be distributed to meet individual and collective needs. The group worshiped together, gathering in one or another of their homes. They considered their move to Reba Place a break with the Mennonite church, but they remained faithful to their Anabaptist tradition.

There was almost no formal structure to that early group. They were together every day, discussing their problems, dealing with cares and troubles as they arose, playing and celebrating whenever they could. It all happened so easily that no structure was needed. They were small enough that whenever some decision had to be made, they would all simply gather and discuss it.

For over ten years Reba Place Fellowship remained remarkably stable. It was small, its organization the simplest. And because all the members came from the same background and shared many common assumptions and values, there was general agreement not only in the broad meaning of their life together but in many of its details as well. Then, too, because they knew of no contemporary experiment quite like their own, they had no idea what to expect and so expected very little. Community life was a series of gifts to them—love, support, togetherness—gifts they had hardly anticipated. Even when their number suddenly doubled in 1969 when a group that had been associated with the Church of Hope in Chicago joined them after their church was taken way, Reba Place Fellowship continued unchanged.

The second stage came in 1971 when Virgil Vogt, who with his wife and five children had been a member of Reba Place since 1960, went to a charismatic conference led by Graham Pulkingham at the Church of the Redeemer in Houston. He was so impressed with what he saw, with the spirit that seemed to fill all who attended, that he asked Graham Pulkingham to visit Reba Place.

Pulkingham did in 1972. He was with the group for one week and in that time something remarkable happened. All who were there then remember the week as one when they discovered how really much God had given them and yet how much more God still offered. They all came to feel—truly feel—the Spirit working in their lives. Many also found that through the gift of the Spirit they were able to heal others, heal their physical ills, their mental and their spiritual ills. There were cures then that even a few days before they would not have believed possible.

Finding that with the help of the Spirit they could expect more of themselves, they began to expect more from their community as well, and very soon after its second, Reba Place began its third stage. It began to change from a community made up of a collection of separate families living in their own homes or apartments to households made up of several families.

Some of the households, particularly those made primarily of singles, grew quite large—often over two dozen. Reba Place was growing rapidly during this time, attracting many new members, most of them young people who discovered there a love, a determination to bring about a better world, and a Christian dedication that gave their lives a refreshing and startling new meaning. These new members often came together to live in one house, sharing cooking, cleaning, and prayer. Other households were smaller but often included two or more entire families.

In 1976 the community underwent yet another change when it officially joined both the Mennonite and the Brethren churches. Although strongly identifying with their Anabaptist heritage, the members of Reba Place had had no formal ties with any denomination since 1957. Again, it was Graham Pulkingham who urged them to make this connection. Both of the churches they joined upheld the Anabaptist ideas and doctrines with which they had always identified, and with two memberships they hoped to keep themselves from becoming too narrowly sectarian. They had always seen themselves as an ecumenical movement that took its inspiration from, but did not intend to limit itself to, one tradition. By joining two denominations they sought to emphasize both their Anabaptist past and their hope for an ecumenical future.

But also about this time there were signs that they might have been moving too quickly. The movement from separate homes to households of many different families had begun in 1974 and by 1976 included nearly everyone. The households made up largely of singles remained strong, but in those with two or more families, particularly families with small children, problems were developing.

Allen and Jeane Howe were part of the first group to form a household. Theirs was relatively small, two families, the Howes with their young son and daughter and another family with a daughter the same age as the Howe's. At times others stayed with them as well. They lived as one family, cleaning together, cooking together, eating their meals together. The two girls shared the same bedroom so they were even raising their children together.

"We found it very hard to live that close," Allen said. "Even in the most tightly knit families there are strains and tensions that come naturally from people living together. Put several young families that close together and those tensions multiply many times over."

Jeane Howe explained: "It was the routine matters that were usually the ones that caused the most problems. The way the food was cooked, what sort of things should be bought that week, what time we should eat—all of these were areas where we found ourselves frequently disagreeing. Then, of course, there were the children. Each set of parents had different ways of raising their children. That had never been a problem when we were neighbors, but living in the same house it just didn't work.

"Each of us began to find many little weaknesses and insecurities in ourselves which we had not suspected or, if we knew of them, had been able to control. In the pressure of the household many of these came out. Finally when Allen and I found that the strain of living in household was hurting us as a couple we asked to move out."

They had been the first ones to try household; they now became the first ones to leave it. The Howes' request came when nearly everyone else was living in households. At that time no one understood what could have gone wrong.

"We had all invested ourselves very deeply," Jeane said. "It was a profoundly painful experience to feel that the household was not working and even more painful to have to ask to leave. There was little appreciation in the general community at the time of just how much households demand of a person. Our leaving could have been handled with more sympathy and care than it was—it would be handled better today."

In the coming months, however, what the Howes had gone through was experienced by many others in household after household. Reba Place reached a fifth stage when households came to be seen as something to be approached thoughtfully and carefully. It was a hard lesson, and when people talk of this time it is in a somewhat quieter tone, the deep pain of the experience still present in their voices. A community less firmly united than Reba Place might not have survived so much tension and disappointment, but it did survive and in many ways became stronger.

The community seems to have come out of the experience with a heightened respect for the nuclear family as a distinct unit. There are still households, but they are made up mostly of singles, the couple in charge usually one whose children have grown. Families with young children are encouraged to direct their attention more to their own needs, and the families that do open their homes usually limit themselves to including one or perhaps two other people, an arrangement that has proven to be far less demanding than trying to merge the routines of entire families.

To live at Reba Place Fellowship is to become deeply involved with the lives of others. There is an intimacy that may seem strange and perhaps uncomfortable to those used to a more impersonal society. The community concerns itself with its members and considers as its own each member's spiritual, economic, and personal needs.

Wendy joined Reba Place Fellowship nine years ago when she was in her early twenties. Jerry joined several months later. Both lived in a large household with several other singles. Within a few months Jerry and Wendy began to feel a growing interest in each other. Once that had been acknowledged, they went to one of the older members of the Fellowship for guidance. With the community's supervision they began their courtship. Courtship is not a word used often these days, and yet here it applies. Once the speciality of their friendship was known, their relationship was given a certain structure—one very loose and informal, but one where certain things were allowed them as a couple and others denied.

Wendy and Jerry have now been married seven years and have a small child, Adam. As Wendy sat on the floor dressing Adam for bed I asked her if this structure given by the community had intruded on their romance.

"Not at all," she said. "I was grateful for the guidance and counsel I received. I had ended a relationship before I came into the community and felt uncertain whether I wanted anything like it again. What the Fellowship gave to Jerry and me was an opportunity to explore our feelings about ourselves and each other with another person who could offer advice and help us to keep going one step at a time so we wouldn't find ourselves moving any faster than we both wanted.

"With the help of the community our love was allowed to grow at its own pace so that from that love could bloom a mature relationship. It also helped tremendously that we were living in the same household. That allowed us to spend long hours together doing day-to-day things such as washing, cleaning, cooking—all the time learning a great deal about each other. After we were married there were very few of those problems of adjustment so often experienced in the first year or so. We had worked them out already."

While Wendy talked Jerry had been in the next room adjusting the crib. He returned, picked up a toy that Adam had tossed across the room, and sat down. When I asked him how he felt about the structure the community had given to their relationship, he agreed with Wendy. He also was grateful for it.

"Do all the young couples who came to know each other here feel as you do?" I asked.

Jerry smiled. "I haven't heard any complaints." He paused for a moment and considered. "In all honesty," he said, "I believe all feel just as Wendy and I feel—thankful for the community's guidance. I know it sounds strange. Many had all sorts of relationships before they came here. They were tired of what had gone before, tired of the emptiness and loneliness and pain that they always ended with. They really wanted help finding what a Christian relationship could be, and how that could be the foundation for a Christian marriage. It is something I know they—as I—will always be glad they had."

I asked whether it was harder to maintain their commitment to the community now that their child was born.

"There is no question that a small child takes a tremendous amount of time," Wendy said. "The community takes time too. And Jerry's job as a hospital counselor is highly demanding, both physically and emotionally. Yes, we have had to withdraw in our commitment somewhat. At this period in our life we simply cannot give to it as fully as we would like. The community recognizes this and respects it. Jerry and I lead one of the smallest of the Small Groups. We asked that it remain small. We also asked that neither Jerry nor I be given responsibility for any heavy counseling, that anyone who feels the need for that care be helped to find it with one of the other groups. Before Adam was born we did much more. When he is older we will do more again. Right now our concerns are more immediate.

"One thing that I believe the community has learned in recent years is that it is important for members to recognize and voice their limitations. Trying to give more than you legitimately can will hurt you and hurt others. People here care very much about each other and so it is often difficult to admit that they might not be able to give as fully as they want at all times in their lives."

Jerry nodded in agreement.

"That's right," he said. "Its not easy to force yourself to hold back. One reason, I think, is that people change after they come to Reba Place. Weak people find greater strength, while strong people come to value their gifts, develop them, and put them to use. It is so exciting to find how much you *can* do that it comes as a surprise to find that you cannot do everything. You have to remind yourself to respect your limits just as you have come to respect your gifts."

Virgil Vogt has been associated with Reba Place since the beginning. He was among the original group of Goshen students who nurtured the idea and helped it to grow. Although not among the earliest group to move to Evanston (he spent those years as the minister of a church in Indiana), he and his wife had from its beginning considered Reba Place their spiritual home. They joined in 1960 and raised five children within the community. A warm, friendly man, with a small mustache and a relaxed smile, Virgil is one of the three senior Elders. He works for the community full-time from an office in the basement of his home.

At one point as we talked he tried to summarize the ideas that had inspired Reba Place's beginning and continued to hold it together:

"First, I suppose, is the belief that God has something to say to us in everything we do. This is an Anabaptist idea. To be close to the Lord means that life is not divided between 'Holy' and 'ordinary.' It is not separated into the time at church, say, when we are with God, and those other times at home or at work when God is somehow not involved. Everything is both. It is ordinary because it is part of our lives, but it is also holy because it is from God and for God. Reba Place is here because a group of people found and continue to find that God is part of their everyday lives.

"Reba Place was also formed as a place to be strong together. We all knew that, as powerfully as we felt God in our lives, unless we worked together and encouraged each other, we would eventually be overwhelmed by the emptiness and hopelessness that is so much a part of a world that does not know the Lord. Alone, each of us would simply be one voice singing a song of joy, soon drowned out by the clamor all around. Together we become a chorus, each voice reinforcing the others—singing louder, stronger, and more beautifully than would be possible alone.

"Finally, this Fellowship was formed as a place to share. Here lives touch other lives in a way that really matters. Unlike most churches, our shared worship is only one of many ways in which our lives are intertwined. We are here to experience close contact with people. The trouble is, of course, that people are not perfect, and often living close to people can hurt. Sometimes living at Reba Place means to suffer a great deal of pain—the pain of misunderstanding, the pain of disappointment. For a time we thought that this pain came only because we were still learning our way, and we were reluctant to acknowledge it. Now we are beginning to recognize that in some ways the deepest sharing comes when we become willing to share the pain of being human.

"Perhaps it sounds a bit harsh to put it that way, but no one should enter a community without realizing how very hard it will often be. Unless they do, they will not be able to last past the hard times to find what is of value."

"Reba Place has changed much over the years," I said. "Has it reached a plateau now, a point of stability?"

He smile faintly, then answered: "No, it will continue to change. It has always changed whether we wanted it to or not. It now seems wrong to expect anything else. The Lord seems to draw us a little closer and a little closer. It no longer seems important to ask where we are going. It is enough that we have come as far as we have."

12. Levels of Community

Thank you, God, for those whose lives touch my life. Help me to see in these, the bonds formed so casually, the makings of something greater, a connection, a unity, and a union which is both a solace for the journey I must make and a journey all its own.

Open House Community and Reba Place Fellowship both strive for the fullest possible expression of community. I found much that was beautiful and moving in the way of life each offered, but I must admit that there were also aspects that made me uncomfortable. Their particular form of community did not seem something that would suit my family or most of the families I knew. This was not easy for me to admit to myself. A few years earlier, during that terrible night in Maine when I had held a sick child in my arms knowing there was no one to call, I had felt myself at the brink of the horrifying isolation to which the American family is moving. In these two communities I saw the other extreme. It was infinitely preferable, but still it was not quite right for me.

What I found most difficult about both communities was the position of the family. Although I saw that in many ways these communities enhanced and broadened what the family can do, I perceived other ways in which the family was given a secondary position. Community *is* a way to draw together life on the edge and life at the center. I had seen enough to convince myself of that. But the risk of community, as I had seen it represented, comes when the community as a whole does not fully acknowledge that each family requires time and circumstances to cultivate a degree of separateness and a greater intimacy. The separateness and intimacy of the family are not subversive to community life. They complement it, becoming, ultimately, its source of strength and renewal.

Talking with the men and women of Open House Community

and Reba Place Fellowship, I felt something like envy for the freedom and variety of options their way of life allowed them, and for their opportunity to use their time and energy in ways more flexible and varied than many of us are permitted to do. But mingled with the envy was skepticism. Could the family come to be accepted as a unity with the full integrity it deserves? Both communities take family life very seriously, but in my opinion have not always taken the special precautions required to ensure that the family remain the primary center of care. Reba Place seems to have come a long way in that area: there now seems to be a general acknowledgment within the group as a whole that the needs of individual families must become primary if the total community is to remain healthy (this discovery coming as a result of the several years when all families were joined with other families in households, an experience that almost destroyed the group). Open House Community, too, seemed to be struggling with this issue when I visited. Many expressed a need for more quiet, for more time for care of families and the group as a whole, rather than always caring for those who come and go.

The fact that this issue is being acknowledged so openly is a testimony to the courage and resilience of the community members involved. When faced with the isolation of modern life, they had been brave enough to venture into unknown territories, replacing separation with sharing, distrust with openness, fear with love. Their life became an experiment, one that purposely sought the opposite extreme to that toward which the world seems to be moving. What is important for those of us who are uncomfortable with that extreme to hear is that theirs is not the only form community can take. Sharing all goods in common is not the single alternative to isolation. It is only one of many ways to express community. One thing that became very clear to me is that community is not determined by the manner in which a way of life is structured—by the number of common meals or the actual method of mutual aid or the degree to which goods are shared. It is determined by something far more elusive.

Referring to the early days of Open House Community, Paul Thompson said, "We thought that all we had to do was live together and share our possessions for there to be community. We were wrong. We needed something more." This lesson I, too, had to learn. I discovered that what made these groups of people true communities was an intangible connection binding them together. With that connection they could choose to share freely what they had. It would work as a community. But with this connection they might also have chosen to own things separately and it would have *still* worked as a community. It is the spirit that brings the sharing, not the sharing that brings the spirit.

The choice is not between one extreme and another—between a family living in isolation and separateness, its few members alone responsible for providing all affection, care, and support; and a family sharing completely with all other members of a given community. The true elements of community are internal. They are not determined by how much each has given up or how closely together everyone lives, but by the strength of the connection of those involved. Possessions in themselves have nothing to do with the life of the spirit. They alone do not affect it one way or the other. Possessions become dangerous only if we become so caught up in our search for them that we forget the spirit. It was probably for this reason that Jesus suggested giving them up. But they become an equal danger if giving them up becomes such a preoccupation that this too becomes a substitute for the life of the spirit. Community grows from a group's members' willingness to connect with each other, not from their willingness to disconnect from what they own. What is important then, is the level of commitment to community, a commitment that has nothing to do with how extreme the way of life might be, how much is given away or how much owned in common. It has, instead, everything to do with the degree of connection all have with each other.

It was this understanding that drew me to look at community afresh. I saw that true community is much more basic to the human condition than I had first thought. It is true that the modern family is drifting into a disturbing isolation, but it is equally true that there are important efforts at community-building that are not recognized as such because they seem so ordinary. I have been involved in these efforts, as has perhaps everyone reading this book. The communities most of us are forming probably appear less dynamic than Open House Community or Reba Place Fellowship, but that does not mean they are something diluted or second-rate. They are true communities and must be recognized as such. Only with such recognition will they become all that they can become.

There are actually three elements, three levels, of community. The first element *must* be present. The second builds on that, the third on the second. None demands a specific style of life; all require a deepening personal commitment.

The first aspect of community, then, is that of *forming ties*. This is community at its most basic, but community it is. This is the community that forms whenever a few people begin to gather on a regular basis and allow themselves to learn to know one another in ways that get past the roles that otherwise keep them locked within themselves. Ties are most often formed unexpectedly. A group comes together by chance or with a particular job to do. No one expects anything special and yet there it is, perhaps all at once, the result of a sudden breakthrough—they discover they are sharing more of themselves than they had expected. More often, though, these ties form gradually, the product of prolonged contact, as they did for the group of friends who gathered originally in John Miller's home. They had come together to pray. Only slowly did they come to realize that this had become the basis of a profound interdependence.

This is the sort of thing with which we are all familiar. It may happen between three or four friends—singles, couples, families—who meet now and then for dinner or for an afternoon. It may be that they intend nothing other than to share each other's company, to talk, to have fun. But whatever the purpose, what is occurring is the first level of community, an important level. It need never pass beyond this, never make its members consciously aware of it and still it is community. These connections are important ones and gathering with others in even the most casual of ways to express that connection helps the family by giving it a wider base of support. Whatever network of friends and aquaintances a family has is its community. It does not matter that the group would never call itself by that name. Neither does it matter that the group may never gather all at once, that one set of friends may hardly know some other set. This *is* community. The ties formed here can become an important part of helping members of a family to go back and forth between life on the edge and life at the center.

The second level is that of *joining lives.* The movement to this level is a major transition, although it may be that very little seems to change. All that actually occurs is that the community that has always been present among a group of people comes to be recognized for what it is. It happens when friends who have called each other every day for years just to chat or families who have come together regularly for fun and for the pleasure of each other's company come to realize that an interdependence has long since developed, so that their connection is not as casual as they might have thought. Their lives have grown around each other. The fullness of the life of each one of them has come to depend on the fullness of life of all the others. They see their connection for what it is— community. In doing this nothing has really altered except the group's self-awareness, but that self-awareness can make all the difference. Ties that are not noticed can never reveal their strength, the full power of the support is hidden.

Connections that appear casual and fleeting might be thought to be easily severed. To recognize the ties and accept the importance of the connection is to reveal how much a small group of people can provide in support and strength for each of the individuals involved. It is also to reveal how much responsibility each has for all others.

For some, the realization of the strength of human interconnection seems to them a call to change the way they interact. For Open House Community and Reba Place Fellowship, for example, joining lives meant moving into the same area and pooling fund and resources, but that is only one reaction. Just to see the people whose lives are connected with your life as a community can be transforming enough.

Also among the communities I visited was the New Jerusalem Community of Cincinnati, Ohio. Tracing its earliest beginnings to a weekend in 1971 when Father Richard Rohr led a retreat for teenagers at the high school where he taught, a retreat that left all those present with such a vivid sense of what it meant to live the Gospel, that every life was altered; their enthusiasm soon spread to parents and friends. New Jerusalem is now a Catholic community of nearly three hundred which is held together by two things above all else. The first is simply the recognition that their connection with each other *is* a community. The second is the belief that it is in such community that Christianity was meant to be expressed. Beyond this there are no preestablished structures or expectations of how the life of the community should be lived.

Every year at Easter each member of the community signs a covenant agreeing to renew his or her connections with the group. The covenant acknowledges a person's desire to join his or her life with the lives of the others of the group, but specifically how this is done is left for the person alone to determine. Husbands and wives are accountable to each other. Their lives are so closely intertwined that whatever one plans to do must be worked out with careful consultation with the other. Husbands and wives sign each other's covenant statements, but they are the only other ones ever to see them. Once written, they are sealed and closed to the eyes of anyone else. The important thing is the recognition that their connection is that of a community. What specifically that connection means is left to the individual to determine.

Father Richard Rohr is still deeply involved in the New Jerusalem Community. He is a man who blends a dynamic energy with a deep calm. A young man in his mid-thirties, he looks younger still, almost boyish, even with a beard streaked with grey. He laughs easily and talks with excitement and energy, and it is probably this that gives the youthful impression, this along with a combination of vision, hope, persistence, and genuine human warmth.

"Christianity was made to be expressed through community," he said. "It is in community that it truly blossoms, truly teaches. At New Jerusalem we are not a group of solitary individuals, we are a people, a people with strong ties to one another. Here there are no empty spaces between one person and another. All the spaces are filled. It is love that fills them. But once a person has begun to feel the interconnectedness that can be felt in community, then it is impossible not to feel it with everyone. Once that happens there is no choice, you simply must reach out to help those around you. You must, because the suffering you see has become your suffering, the hunger your hunger. These men and women around you are not separate from you, they are your brothers and your sisters."

He paused a moment, sat back and seemed to reflect.

"This community began," he said in a different voice, "with a simple Gospel lesson given to twenty teenagers. That does not surprise me, because when it is really heard the Gospel has the power to transform. The Gospel message is simply this, that God can love imperfect things. When you have heard this, and, what is more, seen that you are one of those imperfect things that God loves, then you have heard the Good News. And it is with both of these, both God's love and our imperfection, that we build community. Idealism can be very destructive to a community. An idealist really believes that something must be perfect for God to love it. That is not the Gospel. The Gospel is realism. It asks us to enter into who we really are, then realize that this is the person God loves. The Gospel teaches us to love ourselves, not our self-image, and to love those around us as they truly are, not as we want them to be. And once that happens, once a person finds that even in his weakness and limitation—perhaps especially there—he has something genuinely important to offer, and once he finds that those around him, imperfect as they are, have also just as much to give, then it is not necessary to go far to find community. It is forming already."

New Jerusalem is a community for one reason above all others, because it consciously recognizes itself as such. The second level of community is nothing other than this recognition. And just because it seems to be such a simple thing, its power to transform should not be overlooked. This is something to which most people have access right at this very moment. Nearly everyone already has to some degree or another the first level of community. They have friends and extended family, people whose lives are intertwined with their own. To see these not as something to be taken for granted but as a very special phenomenon that enriches and empowers your life—to name it as community—is to see yourself and all those involved differently. And if the group itself is at a point where it can collectively identify itself as this, then the group as a whole will be altered, strengthened. It may be that nothing concrete is ever changed so that to others, it may continue to seem a group of friendships like any other, but something important has been added. It has been transformed.

The third level of commnunity is that of *union*. This is the highest goal of community and is found in small incidents of togetherness, insignificant as these often seem. A hand touched to ease another's sadness; a late morning conversation over coffee; a passing glance between two people in the middle of difficult work where each recognizes in the face of the other the exhaustion he alone thought he felt so that, smiling suddenly, they each return to the work strangely refreshed—these are moments of union. It is when the differences between people are no longer barriers, not because they have been somehow washed away, but because they have become so fully accepted that no one would even think to hide them. Union can occur at all levels of community. There may be times of union on the level of forming ties, times of union on the level of joining lives, there may also come long periods when it becomes a level in itself. It is always something that comes and goes. It does this not because we as humans are so imperfect, but because we as humans have such a hard time accepting those imperfections in ourselves and in others.

At any level, community has the capacity to do two things above all: to help people to care for others and to help them find ways to reach beyond themselves.

Community can provide a context for the love and care of children. It can provide support for families and support between families. Community can also become the network of bonds of genuine and meaningful connections between people who would otherwise be strangers, breaking love out of the narrow shell within which it too often hides and from which it is distributed sparingly to one, two, or perhaps to three other people—breaking it loose to be spent generously and so returned generously. It is in community that the family can be opened in such a way as to include lasting friendships that support the family's own integrity while deepening and extending it.

Community also has the capacity to help people to reach beyond themselves. In some cases it may supply economic support. In all it can provide emotional encouragement which allows some of its members to live for a time on the cutting edge. Either in the retreat house of the Open House Community where a person may be alone for several hours or several days or with the opportunities that the other communities offer to express longing through music, art, or work for social justice, community can provide a chance to come closer to that thunder of creative energy which is both infinitely beyond and intimately within.

Too often it is thought that community is a place where conformity is the rule. In the true community just the opposite is true. Community occurs at that point in a life shared with others when each person is allowed to be who he or she most truly is.

In his book *A Place Called Community,* the Quaker writer Parker Palmer makes the point this way:

Most of us fear community because we think it will call us away from ourselves. We are afraid that in community our sense of self will be overpowered by the identity of the group. We pit individuality and community against one another, as if a choice had to be made, and increasingly we choose the former.

But what a curious conception of self we have! We have forgotten that the self is a moving intersection of many other selves. We are formed by the lives which intersect with ours. The larger and richer our community, the larger and richer is the content of the self. There is no individuality without community; thus, the surprising finding that an affluent suburb with all its options, but without community may nurture individuality less than a provincial village with few choices but a rich community life.[1]

It is in settings where there is no community that the pressure to conform is the strongest. So desperately do people need some sense of connection with other people, that whenever there is no such connection the impulse becomes all the stronger to pretend that there is. Whether demanded or not, people in corporations, students in different groups of a large high school, or workers on a construction site tend to have a collective style of clothing as well as tacitly agreed upon topics of conversation that have little to do with individual preference; these work to emphasize the superficial similarity of those in the group while hiding the deeper differences among them.

Only in community (even if not explicitly recognized as such) are the ties strong enough that individual differences find their true expression, their full acceptance. Within community it no longer need be true that a person can only be privately what he or she is most truly. The ties of community are deep enough that outward expressions of conformity are not needed. In fact, it is the expression of the very part of each person that is unique to him or her that gives community its life. Community is formed when human beings come together to share themselves, and this can only happen when the unrelenting push toward conformity that is so much a part of life outside community is halted and people are allowed to be themselves. It is because people are different that they have so much to offer one another. But only a group with deep ties of love and mutual care can allow those differences to be seen.

Community cannot itself resolve the imbalance of the movement between the spirituality of the family and that of the desert. As with everything else considered, it is only part of the solution. But it does provide a context where the transition back and forth may be made a bit more smoothly, a stage where the steps of the dance that joins the two ways of life may be practiced. And what community means here is not something alien, not something that necessarily demands a radical alteration of the structure of life. It is a way of being connected with others and, beyond that, of acknowledging that connection so that there might be moments when all see that it is God, not empty space, which fills the distance between people.

13. The Magnificent Dance

A week after his birth—the birth that followed the night of the fireflies—our oldest son was baptized. Family and friends crowded into the living room of the baby's grandparents, where the baptism would take place. All four of the child's grandparents were there, as were his many aunts and uncles (all of whom were just getting used to the new title) and many friends.

A few found chairs. Some sat on the floor. Many stood. The priest stood in the center of the room. All grew quiet.

Pamela and I came to the door holding the child, the godparents behind us. The priest welcomed us.

"What name do you give your child?" he asked.

"Nathan Paul."

"What do you ask of God's Church for Nathan?"

"Baptism."

It was then that we, first the parents, then the godparents, promised to care for the child, to help him grow, to nurture him in faith and in love. There was a reading from Paul's letter to the Romans:

Are you not aware that we who were baptized into Christ Jesus were baptized into his death? Through baptism into his death we were buried with him, so that, just as Christ was raised from the dead by the glory of the father, we too might live a new life. If we have been united with him through likeness to his death so shall we be through a like resurrection. (6:3–5)

In place of a homily, different people about the room, anyone who wanted, talked about what this moment meant to them and what they hoped for for the child. Then, after the moment of silence that followed, Pamela stepped forward and removed the child's cap. The baptismal font was a porcelain washbowl and pitcher that had been in the family for generations. Carefully the priest poured the water on the baby's head and prayed. The child began to whimper.

The child was then anointed on the crown of the head with oil and clothed in a white robe.

On the table beside the priest a candle burned.

"Receive the light of Christ," the priest said.

I stepped forward and lit a second candle from that first as the priest continued: "Parents and godparents, and all in this room, this light is entrusted to you to be kept burning brightly. This child of yours has been enlightened by Christ. He is to walk always as a child of the light. May he keep the flame of faith alive in his heart. When the Lord comes, may this child go out to meet him with all the saints in the heavenly kingdom."

A guitar was brought out and a song sung. There was a final prayer and blessing. The service ended, but the celebration did not. Now dried and comforted, the baby had fallen asleep, but all around him were congratulations and laughter.

In the next room the long table had already been set and now food was being carried from the oven where it had been warming. Sarah was there supervising everything. The turkey was carried out, the pasta, the vegetables, and, of course, the bread.

Everyone squeezed around the table. Only Pamela stood apart, holding the baby.

"He's sound asleep," she said. "I should lay him down, but it seems such a shame that he wouldn't be here. The party is for him.

"Wait, I have an idea."

Pamela hurried off and returned with the baby in the small infant seat in which he sometimes slept. She removed the flowers that had been in the center of the table and placed him there, in the infant seat, instead. He became the centerpiece, completely surrounded by food and by the faces of those who had come to be with him this day.

Several clapped. He did not even stir in his sleep.

"That's perfect. It's right where he should be."

The food was passed amid rising talk and laughter. It was a

long, happy, noisy feast and through it all the baby slept.

Life is full of beginnings. For Pamela and me the spirituality of life at the center had had one beginning with our marriage. Here it had another. We were beginning something that was for us entirely new, but we were not beginning alone. We were surrounded, just as our child was at that moment literally surrounded, by a community of people who would ensure that neither our life, nor his, would be one of isolation; rather, our life would be connected with many others in the day-to-day work of love and care.

There would be many to turn to on this journey, many offering help, and that would make the journey easier. But still the journey would be our own. Although there would be solace, encouragement, and assistance, we were embarking on something that would ask of us what little else does: in the months and years ahead we would come to know the long strain and difficulty of a life lived for another; we would also come to know the greater tension that comes with trying to balance this life with that other, the life lived at the edge. And yet, great as the difficulties would be, the rewards were always to be greater.

Trying to live a life that goes back and forth between edge and center is to live off balance. I have not yet found a way to steady the imbalance. Perhaps I never will. But I have discovered that this imbalance can become a dance, a dance of celebration of all life has to offer, a dance of praise for God's many gifts, the greatest of these being the gift of God's love.

The dance is sometimes slow, sometimes frantic. Frequently it is awkward, but it has a beauty all its own. I invite you to try the steps. Reach within yourself. There you will find God. Reach out to others. There too you will find God. Back and forth it goes, until in the end edge and center become one. Everywhere you turn, you meet God.

Lord, bless the imbalance of my days, bless it and turn it to dance. Make it a dance that speaks of the love of man and woman, of parent and child, of friend and of stranger. And let it be a great, magnificent dance, Lord, paced to the rhythms of eternity, a dance of praise to be performed on to the brink of the unknown, and then beyond, into your presence.

Appendix:
Three Services for the Home

Each of these services is intended for the participation of the whole family. Even children just learning to read should be encouraged to take the part of reader.

A Service for the Night. This works well with very small children. It is short and can be read in the child's room just before bed. Toddlers will appreciate the incorporation of the turning on of a night light as described on page 104 as part of the service.

A Service to Welcome the Day. If this is used every day it might be best not to read both the canticle and the psalm but rather to alternate them day by day.

Give this service a try. Nothing draws out the spiritual strength of the family better than gathering together for prayer before scattering for the day's activities.

Inauguration of the Sabbath. This adaptation of the ancient Jewish ceremony is meant to be said at sunset on Friday as the family sits around the table before beginning the evening meal. As always, everyone should participate. It is best that one parent say the first of the blessings of the evening meal, the other the second, to emphasize the equal role of both in making it possible.

A SERVICE TO WELCOME THE NIGHT

Let us thank God for the night and the rest it brings.

God is always with us. God is with us in the day. God is with us at night. It is this God who came to join us as a person named Jesus: "In him was life and the life was the light of the world. The light shines in the darkness and the darkness has not overcome it."

PSALM **23**

READER: Lord, you are my shepherd, I shall not want.
       You make me lie down in green pastures.
       You lead me beside still waters; you restore my soul.

ALL: You lead me in paths of righteousness for your name's sake.

READER: Even though I walk through the valley of the shadow of death,
       I fear no evil;
       for you are with me; your rod and your staff they comfort me.

ALL: You prepare a table before me in the presence of my enemies;
       you anoint my head with oil, my cup overflows.

READER: Surely goodness and mercy shall follow me all the days of my life;
       and I shall dwell in the house of the Lord forever.

SONG: "EVENING"

Thomas Tallis, ca. 1567

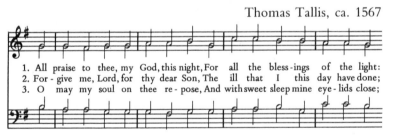

1. All praise to thee, my God, this night, For all the bless-ings of the light:
2. For-give me, Lord, for thy dear Son, The ill that I this day have done;
3. O may my soul on thee re-pose, And with sweet sleep mine eye-lids close;

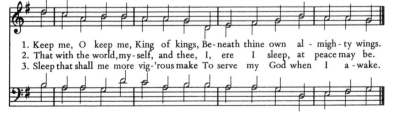

1. Keep me, O keep me, King of kings, Be-neath thine own al-migh-ty wings.
2. That with the world, my-self, and thee, I, ere I sleep, at peace may be.
3. Sleep that shall me more vig-'rous make To serve my God when I a-wake.

[*Join hands for a final prayer.*]

A SERVICE TO WELCOME THE DAY

[Begin with a lighted candle]

The sun has risen. It is a new day and we welcome it. This is the day the Lord has made. Let us rejoice and be glad.

CANTICLE OF BROTHER SUN (FRANCIS OF ASSISI)

READER: Most high, all-powerful, all good, Lord!
All praise is yours, all glory, all honor
And all blessing.

ALL: To you, alone, Most High, do they belong.
No mortal lips are worthy
To pronounce your name.

READER: All praise be yours, my Lord, through all that you have made,
And first my lord Brother Sun,
Who brings the day; and light you give to us through him.

ALL: How beautiful is he, how radiant in all his splendor!
Of you, Most High, he bears the likeness.

READER: All praise be yours, my Lord, through Sister Moon and Stars;
In the heavens you have made them, bright
And precious and fair.

ALL: All praise be yours, my Lord, through Brothers Wind and Air,
And fair and stormy, all the weather's moods,
By which you cherish all that you have made.

READER: All praise be yours, my Lord, through Sister Water,
So useful, lowly, precious and pure.

ALL: All praise be yours, my Lord, through Brother Fire,
Through whom you brighten up the night.
How beautiful he is, how joyful! Full of power and strength.

READER: All praise be yours, my Lord, through Sister Earth, our mother,
>Who feeds us in her sovereignty and produces
>Various fruits with colored flowers and herbs.

ALL: All praise be yours, my Lord, through those who grant pardon,
>For love of you; through those who endure sickness and trial.
>Happy those who endure in peace,
>By you, Most High, they will be crowned.

READER: All praise be yours, my Lord, through Sister Death,
>From whose embrace no mortal can escape.
>Woe to those who die in mortal sin!
>Happy those she finds doing your will!
>The second death can do no harm to them.

ALL: Praise and bless my Lord, and give God thanks,
>Serve God with great humility.

Dear God, light of my soul, you have filled the sky with the light of the sun. We need no other.

[The candle is blown out.]

PSALM 104 (1–4, 10–11, 16–30, 33–35)

READER: Bless the Lord, O my soul!
>O Lord my God, you are very great.

ALL: You are clothed with honor and majesty,
>who covered yourself with light as with a garment,
>who has stretched out the heavens like a tent,
>who has laid the beams of your chambers on the waters,
>who makes the clouds your chariot,
>who rides on the wings of the wind,
>who makes the winds your messengers, fire and flame your ministers.

READER: You make springs gush forth in the valleys;
      they flow between the hills;
      they give drink to every beast of the field;
      the wild animals quench their thirst.

ALL: The trees of the Lord are watered abundantly, the cedars of Lebanon which God planted.

In them the birds build their nests, the stork has her home in the fir tree.

The high mountains are for the wild goats; the rocks are a refuge for the badgers.

READER: You have made the moon to mark the seasons;
      the sun knows its time for setting.

You make darkness, and it is night, when all the beasts of the forest creep forth.

And when the sun rises, people go forth to their work and to their labor until the evening.

ALL: These all look to you to give them their food in due season.

When you give to them, they gather it up;
      when you open your hand they are filled with good things.

READER: When you hide your face they are dismayed;
      when you take away their breath, they die and return to dust.

When you send forth your spirit they are created;
      and you renew the face of the ground.

ALL: I will sing to the Lord as long as I live;
      I will sing praise to my God while I have being.

May my meditation be pleasing to God for I rejoice in the Lord.

READER: Bless the Lord, O my soul!
Praise the Lord.

SONG: "MORNING HAS BROKEN"

Eleanor Farjeon   Gaelic melody

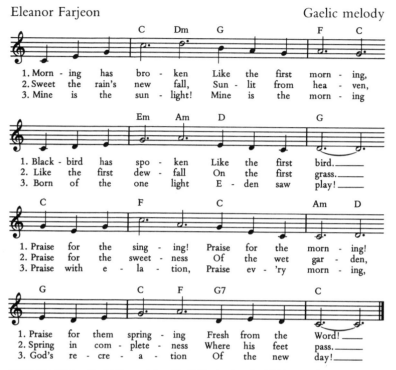

1. Morn - ing has bro - ken Like the first morn - ing,
2. Sweet the rain's new fall, Sun - lit from hea - ven,
3. Mine is the sun - light! Mine is the morn - ing

1. Black - bird has spo - ken Like the first bird.
2. Like the first dew - fall On the first grass.
3. Born of the one light E - den saw play!

1. Praise for the sing - ing! Praise for the morn - ing!
2. Praise for the sweet - ness Of the wet gar - den,
3. Praise with e - la - tion, Praise ev - 'ry morn - ing,

1. Praise for them spring - ing Fresh from the Word!
2. Spring in com - plete - ness Where his feet pass.
3. God's re - cre - a - tion Of the new day!

PRAYER

Dear God, protect us this day. Help us to feel that special love which is your unending gift to us.

ALL: This is the day the Lord has made. Let us rejoice and be glad.

INAUGURATION OF THE SABBATH

Let us now pray in the words and psalms Jesus used as he welcomed the seventh day, the Sabbath. This was a time that he used then, as our Jewish friends have used since, to reflect on the glory of God and of God's creation.

[On lighting the Sabbath candles:]

Blessed are you, O Lord our God, creator of the universe, who has sanctified us by your commandments, and commanded us to kindle the Sabbath light.

PSALM 8

READER: O Lord, our Lord, how majestic is your name in all the earth.

ALL: You whose glory above the heavens is chanted by
    the mouths of babes and infants,
You have founded a bulwark because of your foes
    to still the enemy and the avenger.

READER: When I look at your heavens, the work of your fingers,
    the moon and the stars which you have established;
What are men and women that you are mindful of them,
    and their children that you care for them?

ALL: Yet you have made them little less than God
    and crowned them with glory and honor.

READER: You have given them dominion over the works of your hands;
    you have put all things under their feet,
    all sheep and oxen, and also the beasts of the field,
    the birds of the air and the fish of the sea,
    whatever passes along the paths of the sea.

ALL: O Lord, our Lord, how majestic is your name in all the earth.

PSALM 139 (1–18, 23–24)

READER: O Lord, you have searched me and known me!
You know when I sit down and when I rise up;
    you discern my thoughts from afar.

You search out my path and my lying down,
and are acquainted with all my ways.

ALL: Even before a word is on my tongue,
lo, O Lord, you know it altogether.
You do beset me behind and before,
and lay your hand upon me.
Such knowledge is too wonderful for me;
it is high, I cannot attain it.

READER: Whither shall I go from your Spirit?
Or whither shall I flee from your presence?
If I ascend to heaven, you are there!
If I make my bed in sheol you are there!
If I take the wings of the morning
and dwell in the uttermost parts of the sea,
even there your hand shall lead me,
and your right hand shall hold me.

ALL: If I say, "Let only darkness cover me,
and the light about me be night,"
even the darkness is not dark to you,
the night is bright as day;
for darkness is as light with you.

READER: For you did form my inward parts,
you did knit me together in my mother's womb.
I praise you because you are fearful and wonderful.
Wonderful are your works!

ALL: You know me right well;
my frame was not hidden from you when I was made
in secret,
intricately wrought in the depths of the earth.
Your eyes beheld my unformed substance; in your book
were written,
every one of them, the days that were formed for me,
when as yet there was none of them.

READER: How precious to me are your thoughts, O God!
How vast is the sum of them!

If I would count them they are more than the sand.
When I awake, I am still with you.

ALL: Search me, O God, and know my heart!
Try me and know my thoughts!
And see if there be any hurtful way in me,
and lead me in the way everlasting!

SCRIPTURE READING: GENESIS 1:31–2:2

And it was evening and it was morning—the sixth day.

And the heaven and the earth were finished and all their host. And on the seventh day God had finished the work which God had made; and God rested on the seventh day from all the work which God had made. And God blessed the seventh day, and hallowed it, because God rested thereon from all the work which God had created and made.

BLESSING THE EVENING MEAL

Blessed are you, O Lord our God, creator of the universe, who brings forth the bread from the earth.

[Bread is broken and passed. Each person takes, breaks the bread, eats and passes in turn.]

Blessed are you, O Lord our God, creator of the universe, who creates the fruit of the vine.

[A glass of wine is passed. Each person takes, drinks, and passes in turn.]

Blessed are you, O Lord our God, creator of the universe, who has sanctified us by your commandments and has taken pleasure in us, and in love and favor has given us your holy Sabbath as an inheritance, a memorial of the creation—that day being also the first of the holy convocations, in rememberance of the departure from Egypt. For you have chosen us and sanctified us and in love and favor have given us your holy Sabbath as an inheritance. Blessed are you, O Lord, who hallows the Sabbath.

CLOSING PRAYER [ALL TAKE HANDS AS ONE OF THE FAMILY PRAYS A SPONTANEOUS PRAYER]

Notes

Chapter 1: Life on the Edge

1. Alfred North Whitehead, *Religion in the Making* (Cleveland, OH: World, 1967), p. 19.
2. Robert Gregg, trans., *Athanasius, the Life of Antony and the Letter to Marcellinus* (New York: Paulist Press, 1980), p. 37.
3. Ibid., p. 41.
4. Ibid., p. 42.
5. Ibid., p. 31.
6. Nikos Kazantzakis, *Report to Greco* (New York: Simon & Schuster, 1965), p. 16.
7. Henri Nouwen, *The Way of the Heart: Desert Spirituality and Contemporary Ministry* (New York: Seabury Press, 1981), p. 25.
8. Joseph Conrad *Nostromo: a Tale of the Seaboard* (Baltimore: Penguin Books, 1963), p. 409.
9. Ibid.
10. Whitehead, *Religion in the Making,* p. 16.
11. Ibid.
12. Dietrich Bonhoffer, *The Cost of Discipleship* (New York: Macmillan, 1961), p. 7.
13. Thomas Merton, *The Wisdom of the Desert* (New York: New Directions, 1960), p. 9.
14. Gregg, Athanasius, p. 58.
15. Ibid., p. 47.
16. John S. Dunne, *Time and Myth* (Notre Dame, IN: University of Notre Dame Press, 1975), p. 20.
17. Merton, *The Wisdom of the Desert,* pp. 56–57.
18. Exodus 33:18, RSV.
19. Exodus 34:29, RSV.
20. Gregg, *Athanasius,* p. 81.
21. Ibid., p. 84.

Chapter 2: Life at the Center

1. Anne Morrow Lindbergh, *Gift from the Sea* (New York: Random House, Vintage Books, 1975), p. 81.
2. Elizabeth O'Connor, *The New Community* (New York: Harper & Row, 1976), p. 14.
3. Ibid., p. 58.
4. Lindbergh, *Gift from the Sea,* p. 46.
5. Alexander Marshack, "Exploring the Mind of Ice Age Man," *National Geographic* 147, no. 1 (January 1975), pp. 64–89.
6. 1 Kings 19:11–13, RSV.

Chapter 3: Two Ways of Life

1. Exodus 34:30, RSV.
2. Isaiah 54:2, NEB.
3. Dunne, *Time and Myth,* p. 6.
4. Edward Rice, *The Man in the Sycamore Tree* (Garden City, NY: Doubleday, Image Books, 1972), p. 176.
5. Ibid.

Chapter 5: The Practice of the Presence of God

1. Romans 6:5–12, RSV; italics mine.
2. 2 Corinthians 4:7–12, RSV.
3. Ephesians 3:17b–19, RSV.

Chapter 6: The Sacrament of the Care of Others

1. Malcolm Muggeridge, *Something Beautiful for God* (New York: Ballantine Books, 1971), p. 71.
2. Ibid., pp. 71, 72.

Chapter 7: The Sacrament of the Routine

1. Deuteronomy 30:11b–14, RSV.
2. *Silent Pilgrimage to God: the Spirituality of Charles de Foucauld* (Maryknoll, NY: Orbis Books, 1974), p. 15.
3. Ibid.
4. Ibid., p. 16.
5. Ibid., p. 17.
6. Ibid., p. 29.
7. Ibid.
8. Ibid., p. 20.
9. *The Way of the Pilgrim and the Pilgrim Continues His Way,* trans. Helen B. Bacovein (Garden City, NY: Doubleday, Image Books, 1978), p. 62.
10. Ibid., p. 15.
11. Ibid., p. 19.
12. Ibid., p. 27.
13. Ibid., p. 41.
14. Ibid.
15. Ibid., p. 34.
16. Brother Lawrence of the Resurrection, *The Practice of the Presence of God,* trans. John Delaney (Garden City, NY: Doubleday, Image Books, 1977), p. 65.
17. Ibid., p. 41.
18. Ibid., p. 47.
19. Ibid., p. 49, 50.
20. Ibid., p. 50.
21. Ibid., p. 69.
22. Ibid., p. 68, 69.

Chapter 11: Family and Community

1. Paul Thompson, "Community Encounters the World," unpublished manuscript, pp. 20, 21.
2. Thompson, "Community Encounters the World," p. 23.
3. Ed McNally, *Community Bulletin,* December, 1976.

4. Ibid.
5. Paul Thompson, *Community Bulletin,* April, 1977.
6. Flo McNally, *Community Bulletin,* October, 1974.
7. John Horsh, *The Hutterite Brothers,* Goshen, Indiana, 1931. Quoted in William R. Estep, *The Anabaptist Story* (Grand Rapids, MI: Eerdmans, 1981), p. 101.
8. The Society of Brothers, a twentieth-century revival of the *Bruderhof* community, began in Germany in the 1930s, then fled to this country to escape the Nazis. It has three thriving farm communities: Woodcrest in Rifton, NY 12471; Evergreen in Norfolk, CT 06068; and New Meadow Run, in Farmington, PA 15437.
9. *Concern: A Pamphlet Series,* no. 1, 1954, inside cover.
10. John Miller, "The Church in the Old Testament," *Concern,* no. 2, 1955, pp. 13, 14.
11. C. Norman Krause and John Miller, "Intimations of Another Way—A Progress Report," *Concern,* no. 3, 1956, p. 11.

Chapter 12: Levels of Community

1. Parker Palmer, *A Place Called Community* (Wallingford, PA: Pendle Hill Publications, 1977), no. 212, p. 5.